Men are from Wagga and Women Wish They Weren't

Steve Myhill

Lothian
BOOKS

Author's note

The words in this book were first published, in no particular order, in *Better Homes and Gardens* magazine. It has dawned on me, five years on, that these words constitute a manual for men attempting to cope with the shock of 21st-century life, and a code-breaker guide for women bewildered by the strange thought-processes of their cherished partner.

So for the good of humanity, I've collected my articles, given them a lick and polish (not literally) and put them in a sensible order, I think.

Thomas C. Lothian Pty Ltd
11 Munro Street, Port Melbourne, Victoria 3207
Copyright © Steve Myhill 2000

First published 2000

National Library of Australia
Cataloguing-in-Publication data:

Myhill, Steve.
  Men are from Wagga and women wish they weren't.

  ISBN 0 7344 0140 X.

  1.Interpersonal relations. 2. Australian wit and humor.
  3. Man-woman relationships. I. Title. II. Title: Better homes and gardens.

306.7

Cover design by Studio Pazzo
Illustrations by Jo McComiskey
Typeset by J&M Typesetting
Printed in Australia by Griffin Press Pty Limited

Contents

Acknowledgements

My huge thanks go to all the lovely people at *Better Homes and Gardens* magazine, particularly Toni, Carol and Penny for keeping me honest, and to the best darned cartoonist and ceramic artist this side of the Mississippi, Jo McComiskey. Thank you, Matt Handbury, executive chairman of Murdoch Magazines and all-round nice guy. A special mid-western thanks to Jerry Ward of Meredith Corporation for taking the time to read my column at his home in Des Moines, Iowa.

Massive thanks to Rachel, Rick and Rick Raftos Management, for finding me such a great publisher in record time. Also, thank you to Sarah Dawson without whom there would have been words in this book that weren't quite right — and that just won't do.

Introduction

Men are from Wagga and Women Wish They Weren't is a man's-eye view of life at the front line of the battle of the sexes — the home front.

I want us all to get along, I really do. And as in so many countries around the world, we sometimes need a little help. If your house is an occasional war zone, think of me as your very own UN peacekeeper — a bloke with a cheap haircut and dodgy-looking cap, who'd prefer to be paid in US dollars. I'm here to help, but if you start throwing stuff, I'll bolt to somewhere safe until it's all over.

This isn't a self-help book, but if I can help you to pay good money for it, then I'm sure it'll make you almost as happy as I am. I want to help men feel less ashamed of themselves. You can't help it if you're untidy — it's genetic. It's natural to like a shed, to like using power tools, to become aroused by the smell of exhaust smoke. And women can't help it if they want to talk about 'the relationship'— just think of it as their equivalent of the latest sports update.

I hope that when you've read this book, you'll realise you're not alone. Blokes tend not to stand around telling each other how they feel, but it helps to know that other men are thinking the same things. Which is usually not very much. Which is normal. And okay.

We love our wives, de-factos or girlfriends the way they are. They love us for what we might be if they work on us long enough. We see them as complex creatures who sometimes get annoyed about the smallest of things. They see us as simple creatures who leave the toilet seat up because we know it'll make them angry.

Life isn't getting any easier for suburban man, but it still beats the alternative.

I don't pretend to have all the answers — unlike the bloke who sits three rows behind me at the footy. Although I must be really good at relationships because I've had a whole heap of them.

1
Man and His Magnificent Machines

To understand man, you need to understand that men love things that are man-made. No, I don't mean person-made, I mean man-made. Nature's all very well, but it's what you can do to it with some petrol-powered monster that makes it really worthwhile. A woman sees trees, a man sees chainsaws; a woman sees a lake, a man sees water-skiing; a woman sees a garden centre, a man sees his afternoon ruined.

From the time we boys get our first toy car, the love affair with all things petrol-driven never leaves us. Cars, trucks, backhoes, they really are just toys for big boys. Think about it, girls, your man may moan about having to drive halfway across town to have dinner with your parents, but try getting the keys off him so you can drive.

This chapter investigates that deep emotional need man has to connect with shiny metal things. Of course, a machine could never be a substitute for the love of a real woman — unless it was a really good-looking robot, like Daryl Hannah in Bladerunner.

A cut above

Aussie suburbia on a weekend. Nothing compares with it. The smell of wood smoke, the laughter of barbie-goers and, of course, the reassuring throttling forward and back of lawnmowers.

I love lawnmowers. I love cutting the grass. All men love cutting the grass. Boys love cutting the grass. It's man versus nature with his favourite weapon — machinery. You didn't think it was just coincidence that the first four letters of macho and machinery are the same, did you? The first time most blokes get to feel the power of an internal-combustion engine is when Dad tells them to mow the lawn. Usually you think you're being punished but as you open the throttle and the engine gets so loud you can't hear your mother yelling at you to watch out for the cat, you realise: Dad wanted you to experience this. He's telling you that you're becoming a man. It's a barmitzvah for Gentiles.

The time has come for us blokes to admit it. Cutting the grass is not a chore. For most of us it's the only exercise we get. We can make a performance out of it. We make a point of sighing at how hard it all is as we carry the endless loads of grass clippings to the compost heap. But if we're honest, we like the fact that we can show off our muscles to the neighbours as we deal with the nature strip. We get to point out to our loved ones how much neater the garden looks. And it really is work. You do have to push the mower. And start it.

But face it, fellas, it brings out that same glee you felt as a kid. Here's something that makes heaps of noise and smells of petrol and oil. And you can destroy things with it. Strong, healthy weeds, a quick grinding noise, gone. I never pick up the items you should pick up before you mow. I like the whining sound as a piece of tree or a kid's toy gets given the once-over with the blade I haven't sharpened for seven years.

There's something very Aussie about things rotary. The rotary clothes line — the Hills Hoist — was invented here. And so was the rotary lawnmower engine. Of course, they were less enlightened days. The new technological breakthrough for women helped them with the washing. Technology gave us blokes something that made grass, wood and stones fly in all directions. It made lots of noise — and it was petrol-driven, too.

True confession time. The first lawnmower I bought was a Flymo. A fine mower in itself, but embarrassing in a suburban garden. They do have rotary action, but it's not a big old steel blade that'll cut through just about anything except concrete — and even then it'll have a go. No, the Flymo has a plastic flail thing. And it's not petrol-driven. It doesn't roar when you start it. You don't get a mouthful of fumes. You plug it into the power point, switch it on and it sort of hums. 'Sounds like a Hoover,' my neighbour pointed out at the annual Christmas Eve barbie in our street. 'I heard you out there and said to my wife, "He's hoovering the lawn again." ' I did the only thing I could do without further loss of face. I bought a Victa and moved.

Ahh, the rotary lawnmower is just so dinky-di — mine's a Victa 4-Stroke: yeah, it's red, girls. Not a namby-pamby roller-and-blade mower that leave stripes on European soccer fields and bowling greens. The Victa just cuts any old how. Doesn't matter what way the grass or fallen tree branch is pointing, it'll cut it. And let's face it, most of our lawns are more weed than grass anyway. If it's green, the Victa will cut it.

And it's about the only noisy thing I do. Most people suffer some level of unacceptable noise from the neighbours. I'm no exception. Dogs that go woof in the night. Kids that scream like banshees at six in the morning. Feral teenagers who can afford V8 cars but can't afford mufflers to go with them. The Victa is my revenge. The dog's owners having a barbie? Out comes the Victa. Teenagers a bit hung-over on Saturday morning? Out comes the Victa. Jehovah's Witnesses coming up the path? Out comes the Victa.

And as I settle into the chair to watch a bit of footy, I can counter any accusations of laziness. I can point out the window at the crewcut lawn and mutter about how much hard work it is, how I'm sick of it and I'm going to pave it all over. I never let on what a good time I've had. So, don't admit you love cutting the grass. There are some things that should remain between a man and his mower.

After the beep

The telephone has more to answer for than meets the ear

A lot of people talk about the pressures of modern life. They are forever leaving messages on answering machines, asking you to get back to them on their mobiles so they can tell you just how busy they are. When you do, you get their voice-mail because they're too busy to take your call and have switched off the phone.

Life was no easier for our parents, in fact it was probably harder. Yet I'm sure they were less afflicted by pressure simply because they only had one phone.

I'm not being a Luddite here. I have two phone lines — a modem and a fax, and an answering machine. But you have to use the phone wisely. If not, it will stop being a servant and turn you into a slave. That is, if you're not one already. Are you screening your call right now? Is that a mobile in your pocket or are you just looking for your keys?

Answering machines are essential if you're running a business. But people get fed up with the same old message — particularly if it's funny. You can only laugh at the same joke twice (maybe three times if it's Billy Connolly). Start with a good funny message and you've made a rod for your own back. People will feel free to comment: 'I liked the last one better.' Or: 'So when are you going to think up a funny message?' Show any creativity and your friends will throw it back in your face. Your life becomes a treadmill of inventing new witty messages. You have to change them at least twice a month. Ahh, the pressures of modern life.

I keep my message simple. This means nobody has any expectations of it being funny (if you're a regular reader you'll understand why). Meanwhile, people will leave messages that assume my answering machine is a doctor's surgery. Old, confused people mumble about appointments. Government departments dial the wrong number but still want to contact someone with a completely different name who I know has never lived here. Should I invest in a phone-call to correct their wrong number? Did the little old lady realise her mistake or did she change buses four times to get to an appointment she never made — all with a bad hip? Will the Department of Social Security Special Weapons and Tactics team break down my door one night, assume I am someone else and accuse me of fraud?

Occasionally, I see the red light flashing, press 'Play' and hear someone yelling in a foreign language. What if they're aliens and are telling me to take them to our leader? I don't want to be responsible for a war of the worlds. Should I have a multilingual message to avoid confusion? Another pressure of modern life.

Then there's 'Call waiting'. Has there ever been a ruder invention? It's the whoopee cushion of telecom-munications. Imagine it: 'Mate, you've got to help me, the wife's left me, she's taken the kids, the dog, the four-wheel drive and my best fishing rod. What am I gunna do?' 'Just a minute, buddy, I've got a call on the other line.' What are you supposed to do while you wait for this person to talk to you — write a country-and-western song? Do helplines have 'Call waiting'? 'Okay, don't kill yourself quite yet. I just have to take the call on the other line, then I'll be back to talk you off the window ledge.' 'Call waiting' actually rewards somebody for coming second — and makes you feel second-best for coming first. It's un-Australian, damn it!

Of course, the king, queen and divorced princess of all phones is the mobile. I cannot believe how many people have these things and use them for total trivia. The number of mobile users on the beach this year was staggering. I can only imagine the conversations. 'Yeah, I've just got here. I've put the towel down. I'm slapping some sunblock on. Now I'm gunna catch some rays. I'll give you a ring to let you know how the water is.' Why do you need to tell anyone you're at the beach? Don't you go to the beach to get away from the phone, the has-sles, the pressures of modern life? I know I do. The only reason for using a phone on the beach is to annoy someone by telling them that you're lying in the sun while they're clearing a blocked drain.

In reality, there is no need to feel under pressure. Just unplug everything except one telephone. Answer it if you're in. If you're not and it's important, they'll phone back. It still works for my parents, and they have their health, their friends, a house, a car and eat three good meals a day. What more do you need? Apart from cable television...

'... it's for you'

Home sweet car

Attractive, well-appointed, elegantly elevated; there's no place like the car

In all the time I've been writing my column, I've never really mentioned one of the most important members of the family. No, not Uncle Bert who always wears his bowling cap and smells of Dencorub, and not Billy the fish. This is a much more useful part of the household: the car.

What's a car got to do with homes and gardens? Please, I'll make the connection, just be patient. For starters, you can have the best house and garden in the world, but what's the point if you can't jump in the car and drive to someone else's place to gloat? Also, your car probably has a little house all of its own, right next to yours. It can be as simple as a piece of concrete in the front yard or a schmicko double garage with tiled roof and remote-controlled roller-door. I feel sorry for the trendy, inner-city dwellers who have to leave their cars on the street. Okay, so they can get a cappuccino and organic vegies 24 hours a day, but leaving your car out in the elements is a big price to pay.

One thing I don't understand is the carport. It really sends out mixed messages. It says: 'I'm prepared to protect the roof of my car, but anything that comes in sideways, go for your life.' I don't get it. The only things it keeps off the car are sunlight (but only in the middle of the day in the middle of summer), and rain and hail as long as they fall perfectly vertically. In other words, the carport is as much use as a chocolate screwdriver. I particularly don't understand those carports with extravagant tiled roofs supported on brick piers or timber posts. All that expense for almost no protection. Maybe it's people who don't want to accept that the car is important to them, but want to show the neighbours that they could easily afford a proper garage if they wanted to, they just choose not to.

I don't think it's any coincidence that a lot of new house designs include an integral garage. This way, the beloved car is actually sleeping nice and cosy under the same roof as the rest of the family. Why, if you leave the connecting door open, it can hear the telly and really feel included. And how about keeping some nice 20/50 oil in the fridge in case it fancies a coldie?

I'm exaggerating, am I? Okay then, what do you give

a name, even though it can't possibly hear you? Your car. Why, you even talk to it when it doesn't start first time: 'Come on, baby, you can do it. I'll have you serviced next week, just get me to the game this one time and I'll never use generic spare parts again, I promise.'

If you think about it, you probably spend more on your car than you do on any member of the family. You don't have to re-register the kids every year, insure them for thousands of dollars and pay off loans to own them, do you? If you did, you couldn't justify them. You'd need at least half a dozen children to be able to pull you along in a half-decent-looking cart with power steering and a sound system with grunt. Even then they'd be struggling to make the speed limit unless they were going downhill.

We like our cars to be an extension of our homes, particularly you girls — admit it. There aren't too many guys who look at a car in a saleyard and think, 'Mmm, nice parcel shelf, my box of tissues and cushions will look good on that.' About the only home comforts a man will go for are seat covers — but only if the standard ones are split or stained with one too many spilt milk-shakes — and maybe an air-freshener in a manly fragrance such as Wet Dog or Iron Filings.

Men think of the car as a combined interactive computer game, rumpus room and music centre. In our air-conditioned magic carpet ride, we can listen to old Little River Band tapes, eat junk food off the seats and pretend that we don't have grey hairs and a mortgage. And nobody can interrupt us unless we give them a lift.

There's no doubt we'd all have better-cared-for homes if we didn't have cars. The order of weekend chores for blokes is: 1. Cut the grass. 2. Wash the car. 3. Admire the car. 4. Drive the car round the block to dry it.

5. Anything else that needs doing around the house and can't wait until after the footy.

Cars: can live with them, can't live without them — which is the opposite of what men say about women. Oops, I think I've found the secret of life.

Keep some 20/50 oil in the fridge in case it fancies a coldie

The gadget man

Give a man a gadget if you want to get the job done

If you've ever watched the winter Olympics, you may have seen curling — a very strange-looking sport apparently invented by a Scotsman sweeping snow from his frozen driveway so his wife could slide an Edam cheese to him. (Look in your dictionary, I'm hardly joking!) I've heard it's a popular sport with women viewers as it's the only time they ever get to see a man use a broom.

It's a tad harsh on us guys, but it has to be said: to get us to do housework, you have to either turn it into a sport or give us a gadget. It's no coincidence that it was Joe the Gadget Man and not Josephine the Gadget Girl. A friend of mine decided it was time he made a contribution to the housework. No man ever volunteers for anything yukky like cleaning between the tiles in the shower with a toothbrush. No, he volunteered to do the vacuuming (or, if you prefer, hoovering, which Hoover prefers very much indeed!). So, pleased with his sensitive new-age guyness, he set out to do the vacuuming ... only he couldn't find the vacuum. He'd never used it and had no idea where his wife kept it, and wasn't game to ask.

So if you want your man to vacuum, let him buy a wet-and-dry vacuum cleaner, something he can use outside too. I know it makes no sense, why would you want to vacuum up water? But, you see, we like to know that we can if we need to. Maybe we can vacuum up leaves with it? You're right again. Why would we want to vacuum up leaves? We've already invented a proper man's tool for getting rid of leaves — the weed-blower. It makes an annoying level of noise, is about a tenth as effective as a broom, ten times more effective than using a hose and doesn't collect the leaves, just moves them temporarily until the next southerly buster blows them all back again.

And have you noticed how men like to harness the power of water? By clipping on a simple attachment shaped, not too surprisingly, like a hand gun, we can turn the humble garden hose into a High Pressure Hose. We can use this to clean the driveway, the car, whatever.

Of course, it doesn't clean as well as a bucket of water, some dishwashing liquid and a brush, but it feels so good to use. We don't care how stupid or illogical a gadget is, as long as it's labour-saving and we feel cool using it.

You may have seen those kids who clean windscreens at traffic lights. Actually, they don't seem to be around as much these days but I always used to think that if I was younger I'd feel pretty cool using one of those squeegee things. If they had to use a shammy or an old pair of underpants to clean your windscreen, you could bet cleaning windscreens at traffic lights would never have taken off as a way to make a quick buck.

Speaking of cleaning and cleaning up, I reckon television advertisers have got it wrong with some info-mercials — you know, like the one for the Magic Mop. The adverts run during the daytime. I reckon that men are the suckers who would buy them by the truckload, so these should be prime-time ads. The way to get us to clean the bathroom or kitchen floor is to let us buy one of those brilliant mops with the clever super-sponge that mops up heaps more than a conventional one. And you squeeze it dry by gently pushing on a little lever! It's cool, I tell you, and I want one. Actually, I think you get two for the price of one, so if that isn't a bargain, I don't know what is.

The computer is another fabulous gadget. Those of you who have one may not realise that it has an unexpected labour-saving bonus for women. You can do your grocery shopping on the Internet and have it delivered to your door. How's that for taking the hassle out of shopping? You still have to undo the knots in the plastic bags, but think of the extra hours watching *The Young and the Restless*.

Though there are drawbacks. Don't think we men are going to let you do the shopping when we could be the ones playing on the computer. No, supermarket shopping will be the new household chore every man will want to do. There'll be impulse buying, but then there always is when you let a man loose in a supermarket. Make sure you keep an eye on the shopping bill, because if you get ice on your drive in the colder months, you may find he's lashed out on a whole Edam. So when you're woken by a frantic sweeping on the driveway first thing in the morning, be sure to let your man have the cheese. He might even make it to the next Winter Olympics.

Chip off the old block

There's nothing easy about having the best PC

Technology is a wonderful thing if it's used wisely. If you've read 'After the beep' (page 12), you'll know I'm a tad sceptical about whether the telephone is such a crash-hot invention, but there's no doubting the computer — it's great. And if you don't believe me, ask the richest man in the world, Bill Gates.

For instance, I write my regular column on a computer. When I first started writing, it was on a manual typewriter with a stiff letter 'a'. No matter how much I oiled it, I still had to hit that 'a' harder than any other key. I used to have a pinkie on my left hand which was so over-developed it looked like a bicep. We all flirted briefly with electric typewriters and word processors, but clever people were beavering away making the most labour-saving device since home-delivered pizza — the personal computer.

Of course, men saw the importance of the home computer before women did. That's simply because men relate better to technology, whereas women relate better to other human beings. It's not a criticism, girls, that's why you're better at having friends and children and why we're better at having ulcers and heart attacks. You wouldn't want us any other way, would you?

How many women out there have been persuaded that the family needs to buy a computer to do the accounts and to help the kids with their school work? And how many found that it was just an excuse for the old man and the kids to play video games every waking hour? It may be a lot quicker and cheaper playing a round of golf at home on the computer, but I somehow don't think it's doing such great things for your cardio-vascular system. Although anything that saves a man wearing shorts and long socks is a plus in my book — Tony Lockett excepted.

It's amazing how quickly you pick up the computer jargon about RAM, memory, speed and the like. But more amazing is how quickly your state-of-the-art PC is outdated. It used to be possible to stay fairly current for five years. Not any more. I've had this machine about a year and already it's possible to buy one twice as fast and with double the memory for nearly the same price. That's an incredible increase in the rate of improvement. It's like going from the first car, with the man walking in front waving a flag, to the latest Ferrari, in five years.

If you're the materialistic type, it makes keeping up with the Joneses a nightmare. Not only do you still need the new car every couple of years, you'll have to replace the family computer every year, then every six months, every month, week, and so on. If this rate of progress continues, you'll have that day's computer delivered to your doorstep with the milk. You may think I'm exaggerating and that's because I am.

What I find really strange is that a computer is somehow a more acceptable décor item than a television set. Over the years, furniture companies have spent millions developing furniture to make a TV set disappear into a cocktail cabinet or bookcase. But go into many living-rooms today and the PC sits on a table or one of those awful-looking computer desks, completely out of keeping with the rest of the furniture. Nobody seems to care, least of all the pale-faced teenager staring into the screen, zapping aliens into a million blood-splattered pieces while Star Wars-style sound effects make the six o'clock news seem as if it's live from a war zone.

But new computers certainly come with all the bells and whistles. And games, do they have games! What used to be a box, a screen and a keyboard now has internal fax/modem, 50-watt speakers and a multi-function joystick. Most companies load in so much software that the time the machine takes to boot up recalls the bad old days of a whole five years ago. Your new computer can be a frightening thing, particularly nowadays with those powerful speakers. Whenever a warning window comes up, the sound that goes with it is enough to make your heart skip a beat. But you soon get blasé and ignore anything that doesn't say, 'Move away from the screen, it's about to blow!'

The only other downside of owning a computer is that there's no longer any excuse to send a letter with spelling mistakes, unless you forget to make sure you've set up the spell-check for Australian English and not

American English. (For some reason, Americans use a lot more zeds. Or to be precise, they use a lot more zees.) You can simply set up your word-processing program to correct your most common spelling mistakes automatically, check your spelling and grammar as you go, and the words practically write themselves. And the best bit of all is that it even counts the words, which is very handy indeed when you've got to fit it all onto ...

Out on a limb

It seemed like a good idea at the time

There isn't a man alive who doesn't think he can do any job as well as a professional. The only difference we can see is that the professional does it more often, and makes us pay for something we can do just as well. Which is how I came to be standing on a cold winter's day with a chainsaw in one hand, the rung of a ladder in the other, looking up at the branches of a plane tree. It suddenly seemed very tall. I felt like Jack and his beanstalk and hoped there wasn't a giant up there with a taste for suburban man.

Do-it-myself tree lopping had seemed like a great idea. This tree was far too big for its roots. I could reduce the possibility of falling branches going through the roof, remove the risk of bushfires, reduce the shade over the piece of lawn that dies every summer, and have something to burn on the wood-burning stove. (We must get that wood-burning stove one of these days.)

I reckon tree lopping is just like doing bonsai, only

through a magnifying glass. And instead of tiny scissors you get to use big, noisy tools. I had tooled up with hardware from the hire shop — a petrol-driven chainsaw and mulcher with enough horsepower to keep the most manic of petrol-sniffing rev-heads happy. But up close a chainsaw is a scary-looking piece of equipment. I challenge anyone not to think Texas Chainsaw Massacre when they first pick one up.

Some tools feel balanced, good and righteous when you hold them. Chainsaws do not: they feel imbalanced, bad and downright evil. Looking at one with the power off is bad enough. Fired up, it's an accident waiting to happen. Here's something that, if you sneezed when using it, could probably take both your legs off. If you fell or lost balance, the only part of your body that would be safe would be the arm you're holding it with — and then you could skin your knuckles. That really hurts too. I started to cool on the whole lopping idea when I went up the ladder. People who use ladders every day climb as easily as possums. I looked like a possum caught in a spotlight.

There's a surprising amount of give in a long aluminium ladder. I doubt if anyone over sixty kilos should go up one. And I didn't have time to lose that much weight. The further up I went, the more it moved around. I wondered if I could scaffold the tree instead.

The branch the ladder was leaning against didn't look as solid up close either. What I would have liked to see where it joined the trunk was a big old steel plate connector with some coach bolts. Instead it looked a bit haphazard, like an armpit. Nature is very unreliable like that. If trees had been designed by blokes, the branches would be at right angles to the trunk. I put a few extra knots in the rope to tie off the ladder. I reckoned with a bit of luck, if the branch gave way, the ladder would hold it up.

I then felt safe standing on the ladder next to the branch I wanted to lop. Safe enough to look at it. To remove a hand to touch it, let alone try to remove it, seemed as clever as wearing sunglasses at night. Looking down put my stomach on the spin cycle. Those brick pavers that impress people so much at barbies don't look so clever as a potential mattress when you're five metres above them. I chickened out. I don't want to be a one-armed man. (Not that there's anything wrong with that.) If I ever build up the courage to lop, it will be with a handsaw. I can saw with one hand, hold on with the other and not care if it takes all day. I'll have peace of mind. With a handsaw, if I start sawing my other hand by mistake I'll realise it pretty quickly. When they invent a chainsaw that stops when it feels the hairs on human skin, I'll rethink.

I used the chainsaw to trim bushes at ground level. Even then I was as nervous as a long-tailed cat in a room full of rocking chairs. I was happy to switch off and start up the

'Have you finished yet? I want to carve the roast.'

mulcher. Mulchers are fun and easy to use, just like a paper shredder in the office. They make a great sawmill whine, too.

I hired a professional tree surgeon to do the lopping. Took him most of the day to untie my ladder. I wasn't going up there again — that's one job where you need a professional. There may be others.

2

Nature Boy

A few generations back, men spent most of their lives outside. We were in harmony with our surroundings — growing a few things here, killing a few things there, accidentally starting fires — so we didn't know whether we were here or there. In our world, the sophisticated urban man can leave his air-conditioned house, go into his integral garage, get in his air-conditioned car, drive to work, park under the building and ride up in the lift to his air-conditioned office, without ever having to breathe in any natural air. Good for him, all the more pollen, exhaust fumes and pollution for the rest of us.

Basically, men resent the fact that nature can still hit us with hail, cyclones, floods and bushfires. So the more we think we can control nature, the more we try. We've got technology on our side. Only trouble is, we made it.

Smoke on the mineral water

It's the time of year again to load up the beer fridge, get out the heat beads and fire up the barbie. But it's all getting a bit complicated for us blokes these days. We've moved a long way from the humble beginnings when Homo Erectus returned triumphant with a kill, and accidentally dropped it in the campfire. He was soon chomping on a charred sirloin and complimenting Mrs Caveman on her potato salad.

Barbecues have got — and it wounds me deeply to say it — a bit poncy. I'll get onto the Lite and Healthy menus in a minute, but first let's look at the apparatus, the barbecue itself.

There was a time when a fire pit was considered quite sophisticated. Then, with the Iron Age, came tongs and the barbie-mate. By the time we had evolved into Homo Beer-Gutus, the handy ones amongst us had managed to stack a few bricks one on top of the other and light a fire in the middle ... the first barbecue. This had a grill plate and, of course, a brick wall to stand your beer on. But the principle remained the same: flame (or mostly smoke) versus meat, controllable only by how much wood you put on, how hard the wind blew and how much fat was in the snags.

We should have stopped there. But with the advent of the patio, the balcony and the timber deck, Splade-Age Man needed a more controllable heat source. The barbecue on wheels was born — it even had a lid. Heat beads and firelighters followed. It was at this stage in our evolution that we lost the knowledge to make fire properly. Impatient young men served meat with a distinctive petrol flavour, courtesy of the firelighters.

And we've all experienced that sinking feeling as we arrive for the feast and have a cordial drink and chat before the casual comment from the host, 'I'd better light the barbie.' You look in despair at the pretzels and celery sticks, and know that by the time you're offered anything cooked you'll be gnawing at your own hand, while the mozzies gnaw at your legs.

The evolution of the patio

But despite the delay a real fire causes, the portable gas grill is taking modernisation several steps too far ... too far away from the meaning of barbecue. There is no wood involved and no charcoal, and any attempt to provide flavour with hickory chips is insulting. It's all too damn easy. With such sophistication, the masculine skill of turning the snags just that second too late is lost. I'm sorry, but if you use a portable gas grill you may as well give up on the idea of a barbecue altogether and eat sushi.

I blame the gas barbecue for turning the whole nation to needless barbecue overcomplication and the Lite and Healthy menus that seem to go with it. We've become ashamed of the bloody, smoky, charred, lumps of beef and shrivelled snags we grew up on.

Food cooked in wood smoke tastes great. It's probably the equivalent of eating the flesh of a cow that used to smoke sixty a day, but it's delicious. When it was smothered in tomato sauce, we once believed this to be the quintessential taste of the Australian summer — even if it did have a slight tang of Aerogard. Today's kids think barbecue tastes of teriyaki.

Where once the only choice was steak or bigger steak, there are kebabs of teriyaki chicken, satay beef and chicken, hamburgers, honey chicken, prawns, garlic and ginger chicken, whole barramundi, Italian seasoned chicken, octopus, chicken, chicken and more chicken, not to mention chicken. All we cook is chook and I reckon it's crook.

The problem is that we blokes are now left behind as far as outdoor cooking skills go. Homo Erectus didn't come back with a mammoth, dice it, marinade it and put it on skewers.

It all comes down to our genetic lack of patience. Even an experienced char-grilling man will find it hard to resist chucking everything on as soon as the charcoal is glowing. We start to salivate at the thought of those juicy

morsels and our stomachs disengage our brains. Now we're expected to cook gourmet sausages (apparently they actually have meat in them — it's un-Australian, if you ask me), calamari, soyburgers and chicken sausages. Let me assure you, it can be done, fellas: all the poncy stuff needs is less heat, so leave it till the fire cools down. Yes, and apparently all it needs is a bit of forward thinking. These days you need to be a chef, but I still prefer to be just a bloke in an apron, hanging on to a stubbie for balance.

Pyjamas – embracing the inevitable

If you live in tropical Australia, it's unlikely that you'll know the terror of finally succumbing to pyjamas. We bottom-enders — well, south of Gladstone anyway — have cold winter nights to contend with. You have tropical cyclones.

I'm at the age when the need not to wake with a cold neck every winter morning is greater than the need to be sexy. Still, it's a major adjustment to make. Imagine, then, my horror as I stood in a department store studying the daggiest item of clothing since the horizontally striped, acrylic tank-top.

We all know that pyjamas mean one thing: middle age. There are no two ways about it: wearing a top and a bottom to bed is not sexy, it's not young, it certainly doesn't say 'I am virile'. Not even if they're silk. Not even if they were designed by Calvin Klein. Not even if Elle MacPherson delivers them personally to your door. Silk PJs may have worked in the 1960s for Playboy-founder

Hugh Hefner — but who's clamouring to share his bed, let alone his mansion, these days?

Clearly, the men's pyjama is the only item of clothing forgotten by the mega-million-dollar fashion industry. The reason being that by buying them you make a statement. It goes something like this: 'I am a dag; hear me snore.' Most pyjamas still feature a 1960s-style suit lapel (those of you still young enough to sleep nude, check out *The Man From Uncle* or Bond movies starring Sean Connery). In fact, Oasis (that's a pop group, for anyone out there less hip than me) and their ilk are starting to make a similar lapel fashionable again. But why lapels on pyjamas? I find it hard to believe that it was ever in vogue to wear a buttonhole in your candy-striped, fluff-cotton nightwear.

'I'll be there in a minute with the Seaview Brut, Charlene, just getting a fresh carnation for my PJ button-hole.'

'Don't worry about that Steve, your Legacy badge does it for me every time.'

The only pair of PJs that took my fancy in the department store were a kind of imitation tracksuit variety with elastic cuffs top and bottom. And no give-away fly. If, when I'm wearing these, the house catches alight I can at least rush outside without having to wear a full doona. Then, as the flames engulf the roof and the neighbours and the firemen look at me compassionately, I can mumble about my good fortune at having had my track-suit handy for my dawn jog — or else my hose would have been on display too.

Something else that mystifies me is that, in spite of the sporty look of my all-cotton, made-in-China sleep-wear, the shirt has a breast pocket. What on earth for? I checked all the pyjamas in all possible retail outlets, and they all have them. Is there some sinister link between PJ manufacturers and the tobacco industry? Is the presence of a pocket meant to induce me to slip in a pack of Winfields, just in case I fancy a quick drag when I wake between nightmares of being at work naked except for my pyjamas?

I believe the real reason is that when you start wearing them, you're only one step from wearing pyjamas all the time. You obviously care so little about how you look that, typically, you get up in the morning, pop in your dentures, put your pensioner's bus pass in the pocket with enough money for the TAB and a couple of beers at the RSL, and off you go. Unfortunately, I don't know where to draw the line. If you ever see a tall, grey-templed man dressed in a tracksuit that looks suspiciously like a pair of pyjamas and he's studying a display of pale-blue, knee-length socks, please have me committed to the nearest psychiatric facility. Or at least get me to an RSL.

'Tis the season to be sneezy

Tried all the cold remedies and still snivelling? You're not alone!

It's the sneezing season. Colds aren't called colds because you get them when it's warm. Now is their time, and they're out to get us all.

Dry throat? Watery eyes? I get them too, when I see the price of those so-called cold remedies. There are those who have faith in science and medicine. They're called Pharmaceutical Corporations and they see our winter sniffles as money in the bank. We soldier on, pop pills and shove little nozzles up our nostrils every year to confirm what we've known since we learned that C is for Cat ... there is no cure for the common cold. You can dry it, you can stop the headache, you can be non-drowsy, but you'll still cough and sound as though you're talking with a clothes peg on your nose.

We know that a cold running its course is as inevitable as the next set of bank fees. But there's no reason you can't string the kids along for a few more years. You need that hope when you're young, you need to believe that your parents are almost god-like and can look after you through every one of life's trials. Keeping this belief in them is almost as precious as their belief in Santa. No one wants to be the one to tell a kid that guys who go around in white beards and fur-trimmed red suits in 30°C heat are really struggling actors. Don't you be the one to tell them they're going to have colds for the rest of their lives. They have to believe you can make them better. Of course, it'll be another betrayal they'll blame you for in their teens but, until then, you're Mary Poppins, Merlin the Magician and the cast of *E.R.* rolled into one.

Get out the mixing bowl and towel, and boil a kettle; it's time to teach the young 'uns the joys of inhaling steaming-hot menthol and eucalyptus vapour. This is always a good one, because there's instant relief for the kiddies — if not from the vapours, then from the moment you let them take the towel off their head and they can gasp in some cool air again.

It should clear their nostrils enough until you get them to bed. Then out comes the vapour rub. The pong when it's first being rubbed on a chest is like smelling salts — it'd bring round a boxer who's just been knocked out by Mike Tyson. And you've got to keep telling the little tackers that it'll help them breathe better. The tooth fairy has nothing on you — you're the magician who cures colds, the David Copperfield of catarrh.

Your kiddies also need to believe that you can give them something to stop their coughing. Our parents were geniuses at this, weren't they? Anything hot and sweet to drink featuring honey, lemon or whatever was your favourite cordial. Just enough stuff to give it a weird taste so we knew it was medicine, but sweet enough to overcome our resistance to anything new. So as you hand them a cup of flavoured hot water, say in your most soothing voice: 'This is what Nanny used to give me, and it always made me better.' Kids always think Nanny knows even more than you do.

Today's cough medicines might actually be better than the ones we had. I remember my favourite-tasting medicine actually used to make me cough more, but Mum convinced me that it had to do that before I got better. And sure enough, a week or two later I would be. But what about we adults? Who's going to mop our fevered brows and tell us it's all going to be all right? Don't look at me.

I guess if you're a one-person business you might have to soldier on, but the alarming thing about most jobs is that the company will survive for a couple of days without you. I know it sounds crazy — how could they possibly keep going without you at your desk? Trust me, they will. You can actually take something called a sick day to stay in bed and let your immune system work its magic. (This, incidentally, is what sick days are actually meant for, just in case you thought they were for Christmas shopping or hangover recovery time.)

You'll also be doing your bit for office morale. We all know how distressing it can be to see previously attractive friends show up for work looking as though they've spent the morning peeling onions and sandpapering their noses. It's enough to make you feel ill too, even before they sniffle into a used tissue for the umpteenth time.

If you don't want to suffer at all, your best chance of avoiding a cold is to wear a surgical mask at all times. And do your best to avoid contact with all other humans. They may think you're a bit weird, but hey, they said that about Howard Hughes. And to those of you who sneezed as you read this ... bless you, everyone.

No pressure, low pressure, high pressure, no worries

For we homebodies, there's nothing better than slumping on the sun-lounge in our own backyard. It's so relaxing. The sounds of birds, the rustling of leaves in the trees, the unmistakable hiss-clunk-growl, hiss-clunk-growl as next-door's dog tries to eat their sprinkler. But what's that coming up between the brick pavers? A weed. And another. There's a whole clump under the plastic table. The veg-out will have to wait, there's weeding to be done.

Chemically, of course. The only time-effective way to get rid of weeds in pavers is with a good strong herbicide, preferably one that's banned in all other English-speaking countries and also by the World Health

Organisation. That's your guarantee that it's going to work. So it's on with the face mask, gloves and protective clothing and I'm darting around the patio like someone cleaning up after the French nuclear tests at Mururoa Atoll.

To an alien, or a foreigner from a country with a more live-and-let-live attitude to weeds, I suppose it must look a bit strange. A fully grown man, in early summer temperatures, wearing gumboots, long rubber gloves and protective goggles. And carrying what, to the uninitiated, appears to be a large orange-juice container attached to a metre-long spray gun. All this to spray herbicide at weeds barely visible to the naked eye.

Well, Mr Alien or Mrs Overseas Visitor, it's what we do around here. Because every Aussie male knows that if you're soft on the weeds in November, you'll be fighting them until June. And I don't want my neighbours to see me wipe each weed with a weeding wand. If life's too short to stuff a mushroom, it's certainly too short to use a weeding wand.

But I don't spray everywhere. Some weeds are so close to the good plants that you can't risk the overspray. Anyway, there are some weeds which need a man's touch or hand-to-hand combat. I'm not talking lantana — that's machete stuff — I'm talking jasmine. I love jasmine in the spring. But that's how it tricks you, because for the rest of the year it's nature's own barbed wire, creeping and choking other plants. Right now I need to pull it off the fence — it's getting out of control. So are the white ants in the fence; the jasmine's the only thing holding those few palings together — the rail is eaten through.

A simple bit of weed-pulling then results in some

weekend woodwork — and having to ask the neighbour if I can go into his yard and hammer in nails to fix the palings. The dog leaves the sprinkler and watches me very closely for a while — particularly when I hit my thumb and he thinks I'm telling him to sit. I get back on my side of the fence to discover the grass really is greener on the other side. Better put some lawn greener on before I settle down with the papers.

And it's time to check the sprinkler system — for eggs. Yes, I know it sounds strange, but our irrigation system is the sort with black piping and stalks of various heights with little nozzles. Which, apparently, are a perfect size for insects to lay eggs in. So, during a drought, you hook up the connector to the hose-cock and *phttt* — no water comes out, until something gives and a piece of pipe gives way and there's a fountain of water a metre high. So I unscrew each nozzle and clean it out with a pin. It's as much fun as it sounds, yet strangely satisfying.

Now finally I can relax ... if it weren't for the memory of the redback I once found under a plastic patio chair. Out with the high-pressure hose. Men never brush or broom anything away these days. We use the high-pressure hose. It's easier, less effective and more wasteful, and for some reason we like that. The thing about a high-pressure hose and the underside of a patio chair is that the water doesn't have anywhere to go. Well, in fact, it has ... straight back at you. Not at such high pressure, but with enough to force a change of shorts.

Now that I know I'm not going to get bitten, stung or overgrown with weeds, I can settle back and relax. Just me, a cold one ... and the neighbour's daughter laughing at me over the fence as she appears and disappears about thirty times a minute. She's got a new trampoline. Boing-giggle, hiss-clunk-growl, boing-giggle, hiss-clunk-growl ... and a whipper-snipper starts in the distance. Ahh, the sounds of the Aussie outdoors. You wouldn't miss it for quids.

We shall fight them on the benches

It's the little things which scare us

Humankind is a bit wussy, when you think about it. We've put a man (more than one, in fact) on the moon, we've made machines to move over land, sea and air, and machines which slice, dice and julienne. But really, we're scared. We're scared of death, we're scared of the unknown, but we're most scared of insects and common-or-garden creepy-crawlies.

Yes, macho men with chainsaws are scared of spiders, hate cockroaches, fear mosquito bites. We're supposedly the dominant species on the planet and we spend a fair bit of our leisure time fighting tiny little creatures no bigger than a fingernail.

Take the ant. It has many characteristics we should admire. It has an incredible strength-to-size ratio, brilliant communications and a work ethic which would put the most Protestant Protestant to shame. So do we admire them? Do we live in harmony with this remarkable little creature? Not likely. We dust them, pour scalding water on them, spray them, do anything to stop them coming into our homes.

Then there's the spider. Now, we do have a few

poisonous spiders, I admit. But for the most part, they're just a vital part of the food chain, keeping flies and other insects in their places. Maybe it's their ability to do something that we can't even do with aerosols which scares us. Just knowing there's a spider somewhere in the bedroom is enough to make Herself spend the night on the lounge. Screams from the bathroom usually mean there's a huntsman trying bravely to climb the sheer walls of the bath. I try not to kill spiders — but if it's a funnel-web I usually introduce it to a close view of the Yellow Pages.

And the humble fly. Let's face it, Australia is run by flies. We try to deter them with screens and silly, beaded, coloured blinds in shop doorways. We make them stick to flypapers, we hit them with knock-down sprays, we slather ourselves in insect repellent. Someone, some-where, once hung corks off his hat to deter them. Unfortunately this was photographed by a travel writer and now most of the world thinks we all wear them all the time. Of course, urban Australians, happy under our clouds of pollution and car fumes, can keep flies in check. But once you get out in that fresh country air, flies rule. Have as many corks hanging off you as you like, a blowie's still going to fly into your mouth as you eat your meat pie.

Don't forget slugs and snails. They slide, they dare to eat our flowers and vegies; they must be destroyed with pellets or the kinder, more Aussie solution, in a slug pub — funny how letting them drink themselves to death on free beer seems a kind way to kill, isn't it?

Mosquitoes are a menace too. They are so small, so devious and can carry nasty viruses. So we try our best to put them off. More insect repellent on our exposed bits. And we burn those little scented coils to keep them away — of course, we only have the manufacturer's word for this. If you weren't bitten at least once, you wouldn't bother to buy any more coils, would you? You can take direct action too — the mozzie zapper. But don't buy one yourself or you'll have every mozzie in the street at your back door. No, buy one and give it to your neighbour. Let him have your mozzies and have to listen to that sickening *bzzuttt* every time a moth hits the electric mesh which, let's face it, is what moths do.

Now there's another one, moths. They eat our clothes so we make our clothes stink to high heaven to discourage them. Their larvae eat valuable Persian rugs — I am ever-vigilant with the camphor.

However, we save most of our fear and loathing for the cockroach. It's really just a beetle. Plenty of insects are dirtier, more dangerous, more invasive. Fleas are harder to get rid of and they bite you; dust mites can be a far greater health risk and there are gazillions of them feeding on your skin while you sleep each night. But we don't seem to mind them compared with the loathsome roach. Maybe it's the way they scuttle. Or the way they sit, antennae twitching, in your fruit bowl. It could be the old scientist's tale that in the event of a nuclear holocaust cockroaches will become the dominant species.

So this unfortunate-looking insect feels the full weight of humankind's wrath. Surface sprays and baits are now improved so that one infected cockroach kills all his mates. We even bomb our own kitchens to get rid of them. It's meant to kill all adult roaches and make the eggs infertile. Clever? No. We've just solved all their overcrowding problems for them at one stroke.

3

Home Sweet Home

If there was ever a hotbed of intrigue and emotion, it's the family house.

It should, by definition, be where we feel most at home. Yet it only takes the smallest thing to make us feel like we've been abducted by aliens.

This chapter looks at a few of the things that make us want a roof over our heads and regard our home as our best-ever investment — unless you've got a red Italian sports car or make a killing on high-tech stocks.

A clean swoop

I love kerb-side clean-ups. Not Ian Kiernan's 'Clean Up Australia Day' — the less environmentally sound, but more interesting collections by local councils when, if you're like me, you find your neighbours' throw-out things that would take pride of place in your living-room. A lot of councils provide this service, usually four times a year. It's a great time to prune your garden. But try to delegate that to someone else in the house and take a leisurely stroll around the neighbourhood to see what's on offer on other people's nature strips.

There are a lot of experienced scavengers whose whole year revolves around these days. You probably read the story of a couple of ladies cruising the streets of Adelaide, seeing what appeared to be a discarded microwave oven at the side of the road. They stopped, put it in the car and drove off, only to be pulled up minutes later by a police car. It's hard to guess who would have been more embarrassed, the women for taking the police radar trap, or the police for letting them.

A friend of a friend — really, this is true, not one of those suburban myths — saw a nearly new television that had been thrown out. He picked it up and consulted a TV repair man who told him the set was only a year old but needed a new tube, probably $400 worth of repairs. So the friend of a friend — let's call him Chris, seeing as it's his real name — phoned the television manufacturer and said he was outraged that the tube needed fixing on the set that was only bought a year ago. You guessed it, he got a new tube for nothing!

I once had a broken vacuum cleaner disappear from my nature strip before the council contractors could get to it. I can't fix electric motors, but for someone who can it was a gift. I feel stupid that someone got the better of me. I bet that every time they vacuum their house they have a chuckle at my expense: 'I can't believe he threw it out! All it needed was a grommet fuse bush-connector! Look, it can still pick up a bowling ball!'

If you're unlucky enough to live in a neighbourhood full of people like me, all you're likely to find at clean-up time is a few rose thorns and a washing machine that

I recommend daylight reconnaissance, so that you can return for an after-dark collection

the rust just couldn't hold together any longer. Don't despair! Just travel to a well-to-do neighbourhood, where people buy-in specially for clean-ups so they can throw out stuff as good as their neighbours.

I recommend daylight reconnaissance, so that you can return for an after-dark collection. This looks most natural if you have a dog to walk or a pram to push. Dispense with such play-acting if you're the lucky type who isn't embarrassed by lifting other people's rejects from in front of their homes in broad daylight. You'll really clean up!

A friend with teenage children encourages them to do the scavenging for him. It didn't go too well the first couple of years — such was their enthusiasm that he had to hire a trailer to take the surplus rejects to the tip. But those kids can now spot a decent piece of furniture whilst roller-blading past at 60 k/ph. The family TV sits proudly on a salvaged cupboard that to my eye looks antique.

Finding a use for an item somebody else doesn't want should fill us with pride, not shame. It's your personal contribution to reducing land-fill. Worth remembering when you're caught by car headlights as you carry home a neighbour's sofa-bed.

They can spot a decent piece of furniture whilst roller-blading past at 60 k/ph

Head for the shed

If your man's handy, chances are he has a shed, or two, or three

Man cannot live by bread alone. But he can live in his shed alone and, if you're not careful, he will. You may not even realise he has a shed ...

Your garage may be, in fact, a shed. If it's too full of beer fridges, workbenches, lathes, shelves of old jars labelled 'screws, wood' and 'nails, masonry', and tins of paint even to park a mountain bike, what you have is no longer a garage. It's a shed with a really big front door.

Men can no more resist having their own private area smelling of oil and iron filings than dogs can resist fouling next-door's nature strip. It's a territory thing. The shed starts out as a place to park the lawnmower but then you notice that he is spending more and more time at the hardware store and there's constant banging, sawing, drilling and swearing coming from the little box at the bottom of the backyard.

One day you venture in to get the secateurs, and there it is. A cubbyhouse for big boys. His own interactive virtual-reality workshop where he can pretend to split the beer atom and imagine that with a bit more space he really could build a Porsche.

If you let him have a shed, it will minimise arguments over home furnishings. He's more likely to accept the pink floral lounge suite if he can go and slump in his old rocker recliner in his playhouse. If he doesn't have a shed, keep an eye out for the symptoms. He may become depressed. He'll fight over every decorating decision. He'll want to do everything himself, just for an excuse to make a mess.

Or he may create a shed by stealth. Impossible? Think about it. The space under the house that's there because the block slopes — does it have a power outlet that a portable light can be plugged into? Perhaps there's an area with some old plywood that looks suspiciously like a floor, with a few rickety shelves around it? It's a shed. You thought it was storage space; he's turned it into a workshop.

I grew up on a dairy farm. My father has more sheds

You are now entering the plywood zone

than you could schedule. Cow sheds, stables, tractor sheds, trailer sheds, sheds with no name and no apparent purpose. So what did I do? I leaned sheets of corrugated iron up against them and created my own sheds. These, depending on my age and my current favourite TV show, were variously Bomber Command HQ, the escape tunnel in *Hogan's Heroes*, and Fort Apache. I don't think we blokes ever grow out of this fantasising. If you ever approach the shed and hear his voice saying, 'I know nothing,' in a German accent, cough loudly and pretend to be deaf.

So have I got a shed? A shed? I've got four! One is my garage. There's the area underneath the house, ear-marked for a wine cellar. The backyard has a fine old fibro monstrosity founded not on concrete but on rock, like a shrine. And last and definitely least, there's an aluminium prefabricated one with chicken wire on one side and providing half the roof. Okay, some people would call it an aviary, but it's where I keep the lawnmower.

The best shed I ever saw belonged to Chilo, a friend of my father. He was wildly eccentric and had such a stormy relationship with his wife that he kept his money buried in the backyard, fearing she could get her hands on it if he banked it. But he could do anything in his shed. Fix car radios — the first one I owned was repaired in his shed — recondition a gearbox or make any size nut and bolt required to fasten his home-made car parts. If there'd been a nuclear holocaust, he'd have gone to his shed, waited until the wind had died down, then got on with the job of putting a car together with whatever hadn't melted or blown away.

Even as I write this, I can hear a neighbour drilling in his shed, just over the back fence. It's Sunday afternoon, the suburbs are snoozing and he's in his favourite place, making something. If you want to get ahead, get a shed.

How to enjoy the perfect summer's day

The secret is to be sure not to overdo it

Summer is not the time of year to be overdoing it. If you do too much, you sweat, dehydrate and are well on the way to heat exhaustion. Summer is nature's way of telling us to slow down. Which is strange, because everything else that lives seems to speed up.

I wonder why we don't grow seasonally, like plants. It would make growing up so much easier. You'd buy winter clothes for your kids and they'd fit perfectly all winter long. Then, when they're back into shorts for summer, they could grow as much as they like — no need to let down trouser legs or skirt hems. Parents would save a fortune on clothes. If your children were getting too tall, you could make them spend summer in the shade. Likewise, a short winter break up north would soon add a couple of centimetres.

I wonder why we don't grow more hair in winter and less in summer like most animals. Think of the savings in haircuts.

I digress. I'm here with tips on how to have the perfect summer's day. You will need:

Weather

Cloudless blue skies, a light breeze, a touch of wood smoke from a neighbour's barbecue, and high fire danger.

Sunblock

The days of thinking a tan means sun protection went out with the Leyland P76 and the Sex Pistols. Anyone wearing what used to be called a healthy glowing tan is likely to be an English tourist. Soon, instead of Bronzed Aussies we will be known as Alabaster Aussies.

A hat

Very important for the follicly challenged male and the teenager with a buzz cut. It should ideally have a broad brim and SP factor 15 or more. But try making teenagers wear their baseball caps the right way around. They'd rather squint into the sun with their hands shading their eyes. Stops them burning the backs of their necks, I suppose. The older you are, the better the hat you can wear and just not care. Personally, I wear a straw stetson that makes Molly Meldrum look intelligent by comparison. My partner's favourite straw hat would look better on a donkey, but will she listen? She has the right attitude to the sun for someone with an Irish complexion — she treats it like radioactive waste.

A shirt

Who says Hawaiian shirts are daggy? You wouldn't say it to Danno of *Hawaii Five-O*, that's for sure. Linen is cool, as long as you're not the one having to handwash it (not tumble it, not spin it) and dry it flat in the shade. This is a washing instruction which makes no sense whatsoever; the only place I know which is flat and in the shade is the kitchen floor.

Shorts

This garment was so called because the legs are short. Not any more. Now that it's a fashion accessory, the defining thing about a modern pair of shorts is that it is anything but short. Some still allow a manly flash of kneecap, but most teenagers wouldn't be seen dead in shorts which end any higher than mid shin — the kneecap is about where the baggy crotch comes to. The only place a man can still wear his short shorts without being laughed at is playing Aussie Rules or in his backyard. Which is why the ideal place to spend the perfect summer's day is the backyard. So mat the hairs together with sunblock and let the legs breathe. One day you may care so little about fashion that you'll wear powder-blue crimplene shorts and long socks — and think you look good.

Sunglasses

Very important if you're to avoid cataracts in later life. Wear silly little John Lennon ones at your peril. The sun gets all around the frames and you end up squinting (see 'A hat', page 53). I prefer my sunglasses to look like a pilot's or an ASIO agent's. The Cancer Council's wraparound glasses are very good if you really want your kids to giggle and do Roy Orbison impressions all summer.

A deaf ear

Not really deaf, just selective. You do want to hear the sounds of an Aussie summer: cicadas, crickets, kooka-burras, parrots, cockatoos. You don't want to hear whingeing kids, barking dogs, lawnmowers and chainsaws. Best stick in the earphones and listen to the cricket — you didn't think I meant those noisy little insects, did you?

A blind eye

Nothing spoils a relaxing day more than guilt. Only watch the grass grow if you can ignore how fast the stuff rises. If you think it's one of nature's miracles, that's good. If you think you've got to cut it before you can relax, turn your sun-lounge so you can't see it, and have another beer.

I'd give you some more tips, but frankly it's a perfect day outside and this is too much like hard work.

A time to give

Women think that men are bad shoppers, but the truth is that we need pressure to perform

It's three shopping days to Christmas. The womenfolk have been looking for gifts for what seems like a month of Sundays, and now the chips are down. You've got to shop, and fast. But where and how and what for? Easy. Remember what you got when you were a kid and give as you were given to.

If you go to more than five shops you're doing something wrong. Kids' presents are the most important at Christmas. My advice is to go to a big toyshop. If you're buying for your own kids, think what your parents gave you. The great 'Can I have a pony?' campaign of '63 didn't get you a pony, did it? But you still love your mum and dad. Get the kids their second-best present; it was good enough for you.

For boys, buy something plastic which is designed purely for death and destruction using a martial art and small-scale weapons. Forget educational toys. There'll be time to educate him when he's asking you to buy him a car. And girls will be happy with any version of that skinny doll that looks like an actress from *Baywatch*, only more intelligent.

If you're buying for nephews and nieces, think back again. Gifts from aunts and uncles became smaller and cheaper as you got older, didn't they? By the time you hit thirteen, it was record-voucher time. You do the same. It's a cinch.

Friends' children? Remember oldies whom we called Uncle or Aunty but weren't really? Now these guys were really inconsistent gift-givers, if I remember right. The worst gift I ever got was from an aunt who, despite having five kids of her own, always gave something five years too young for me. Her last pressie was a sew-it-yourself wallet. A wallet is masculine, I suppose, but sew-it-yourself? This is no way to mess with the head of a sixteen-year-old. Unless the last time you visited his parents, the same kid stuck chewing-gum under your wiper blades.

If your kids are married off, the next port of call is the department store. If you reckon it's time for grand-kids, drop a subtle hint with the gift; baby clothes or books of the *How to be a Good Parent* variety get the message across.

And if the son- or daughter-in-law has not been for-given for stealing your little baby away, Christmas is the time to remind him or her. A friend of mine once received a case for his glasses from his mother-in-law. When he pointed out that he didn't wear glasses, she told him not to be so ungrateful — she couldn't be expected to notice everything about him. If you're under too much time pressure to be inventive, I suggest a cross-stitch kit for the son-in-law and a multi-blade screwdriver for the daughter-in-law.

If your parents are alive, nothing says it like alcohol. In the case of your mum, the alcohol should carry a fragrance and come in a delicately shaped perfume bottle. Add a framed photo of the kids taken on the one split second of the year they sat still, and she'll think it's Christmas. Which of course it is, poor dear — she gets confused, doesn't she?

So it's off to the third shop on your exhaustive one-day shopping frenzy — the bottle shop. For Dad, his favourite alcoholic beverage. If you don't know it, get your own favourite. After all, you'll be drinking it with him when the Christmas Day fights kick in. If he doesn't drink, get him a hobby to keep him occupied. My cousin, who keeps finches for a hobby, bought my uncle a breeding pair of finches — there was much bonding of the generations as they built an aviary together. And they now have something to talk about. It doesn't have to be wildlife, just something time-consuming and preferably outdoor — like a saltwater pool. Exit shop four.

Give as you were given to when you were a kid

And finally, your partner. For the woman in your life there are two sorts of gifts. Gifts for you and gifts for her. Gifts for you are things like steam irons and dishwashers. Gifts for her are perfume and jewellery. And gifts for you and her are things like camisoles and French knickers — the gifts that keep on giving. I know which I prefer ... if you've ever sewn your own wallet, you'll appreciate the delicate stitching on silk underwear.

True brew

It isn't just a drink any more, it's a lifestyle

There's one thing without which no home is complete. A roof, I hear you shout. Certainly, in a purely physical sense the roof is very important, but I'm talking about something that turns a structure into a home. Television! Close, but no free cable subscription. Kids! Desirable but not essential. It's coffee.

This tasty little bean is increasingly making our world go round. If you live in one of the inner suburbs which are currently being bought up and renovated by young couples, you will be very familiar with coffee. In fact, the only businesses in the main street of these up-and-coming areas are coffee shops and picture framers — two career options they didn't tell us about when we were at school.

Coffee is much more than a drink these days. No barbie is finished until you've had one. Some of us — I confess — can't wake up without one. People actually meet only 'to have coffee'. (The pretence is that it's to have a conversation too, but in most cases it's just to get close to a skilled coffee professional and his or her gleaming, hissing, espresso machine.)

If it's so good, you ask, why was it called 'The Devil's Brew'? Please, that was centuries ago. People who called it that thought potpourri was a cure for bubonic plague! I'm not denying it's a stimulant, but if you don't have blood pressure-problems and only read the favourable medical research, it's actually good for you. There's certainly no denying it has powerful laxative properties.

I'm sure part of the reason for coffee's increased popularity is the intimate relationship between coffee and chocolate. The after-dinner mint tastes good with no other beverage — surprisingly, not even peppermint tea. Cafés always serve, at bare minimum, chocolate brownies and usually there's a mud cake on offer too. The ultimate combination is, of course, the chocolate-coated coffee bean. A bagful of these and your tastebuds have the party of a lifetime. Sure, you won't sleep for a week, but it's worth it.

And your house sells more easily with coffee. Admit it, a home looks better during an inspection if the smell of fresh coffee is wafting through the rooms. Like magic, it makes you see things through rose-tinted glasses. It's like alcohol only you're safe to drive. So if you're selling a house, get yourself a really good Lavazza bubbling away in the percolator — the way the market has been, it could earn you a few extra thousand. (The buyer could well be one of those picture framers.)

Ten years ago, most of us contented ourselves with the instant, freeze-dried variety of coffee. In fact, a lot of us were tea drinkers. But today there's a lot less jiggling and a lot more plunging going on. I reckon that plungers are so popular because they look stylish; the glass pot with the chrome or gold holder. Let's face it, it's the same way you make a pot of tea but with a really great strainer.

Serious caffeine addicts own a mini-espresso machine. They also dress entirely in black, live in café suburbs and ragroll their walls. They're extremists — don't befriend one unless you like manic phone calls at three in the morning to help with a crossword clue.

I'm a dyed-in-the-wool drip-filter man myself. There's something about it — I can understand how the Japanese make a big thing of their tea ceremony. It takes skill. If you don't get the filter paper absolutely right in the filter, it can fold over and cause a disaster. The water doesn't drip into the coffee, it fills up the filter, washes coffee from the paper and blocks the hole in the bottom. You end up with a filter full of coffee-grounds soup. Only the most desperate would attempt to drink it by filtering it through a sieve. I admit it was a bit chewy but I got it down all right.

Last and certainly not least, there's the percolator — very Italian, very trendy and part of a whole set of equipment. Did you know that there's a special little saucepan for reheating the coffee once it's cold? That's because leaving a percolator on the heat once it's perked isn't a very good idea unless you want a hole in the kitchen ceiling and your percolator showing up on airport radar screens. A friend of mine recently filled her percolator with coffee and left it on the hot plate. After a while, a very strong smell of burnt coffee was all through the house. Yes, she'd forgotten the water. The place still smelled a week later, and not in a good way.

That's coffee for you. Nobody said it was going to be easy. But you know what they say — can't sleep with it, can't stay awake without it.

Man-sized problem

It's not so long since we got by without them

Have you noticed that we are now totally dependent on something which barely existed a generation ago? No woman's handbag is complete without some. All good hotel rooms have a box full of them. There could well be one in your pocket right now. I'm talking paper tissues. Family-sized, man-sized, handy-sized, we just can't get enough of them. Yet not that long ago, we got by without them; instead we had that disgusting patch of cotton called a handkerchief.

I'm not advocating the return of the hanky. A less desirable piece of fabric is hard to imagine, particularly after it's been put to its intended use. Those of you who can remember them will recall a couple of things. You got them as presents, usually with somebody else's initials embroidered on them; and it was considered ladylike to have one tucked up the sleeve of your blouse.

The weirdest thing about the old hanky was the amount of uses it had. You could tie your money up in it. If you were a Pommy at the beach you could put a knot in each corner and use it as a hat. You could tie it around your neck and pretend to be a cowboy.

There were the evil uses, too. Every child dreaded the moment Mum spotted an ice-cream trail on your face, which had to be removed by her spitting on a hanky and rubbing your face with it. For some reason this had to be done in public, with many accompanying tuts of disapproval.

The tissue put an end to all that. They're more hygienic, they're disposable, they don't need washing ... but there's the rub. I think the tissue resents the fact that it's disposable.

Anyone who has left one in a pocket and then included it in a load of washing knows what I mean. A couple of ply of gossamer-thin paper only big enough for one feminine nose-blow can disintegrate into enough fragments to ruin a family's washing for weeks.

In fact, a sure-fire way to sabotage a teenager's social life would be to let him or her rock off to a favourite nightclub, only for the ultraviolet lights to reveal little bits of white tissue stuck all over that cool black shirt or dress. It's hard to look attractive when you resemble nothing so much as a Dalmatian in negative.

Any discarded tissue which isn't safely stowed in a bin will certainly come back to haunt you. You drop one as you're lawnmowing and foolishly think the mower will sweep it into the grass-catcher. Wrong. It spreads itself all over the lawn and has to be picked up by hand. If you try to go over it with the mower again, it spreads to an even bigger area in even smaller pieces. In case you haven't guessed, I hate it when that happens. I wonder how many forests are cut down specifically to make tissues. Maybe there are plantations of special tissue trees; they'd be really brittle, thin, wispy trees which go all floppy and disintegrate when it rains.

Tissues really aren't terribly practical. There hasn't been a tissue made which can withstand two hard snorts from a grown man's nostrils. The man-sized tissue is just a ploy to make you think you're getting something tougher, more practical, more in keeping with the hunter/warrior which breathes within every man. All man-sized really means is that the tissues are big enough for us to unfold with our stubby fingers.

You can't possibly start a box of tissues without tearing the first one into several pieces or dragging a clump of ten out of the top in one go. Whereas the old hanky could be re-used many times a day (disgusting as it may seem nowadays), the tissue can be used once, maybe twice, tops. Tissues are a triumph in marketing over matter. They're an inferior product. You can't wet one and clean your kid's face with it — all you do is rub little bits of paper over their skin.

Tissues come in colours, in boxes of countless different designs. This is presumably intended to help the boxes blend into different décors. In fact, all the artists succeed in doing is making them look like tissue boxes. At least this provides an outlet for all you craft lovers to think up forms of disguise.

Yet there is a tissue that can't be beaten. We first saw it in its lemon-scented genius as the refresher towel at KFC. It cleans grease off your hands like magic; it's wet, yet it doesn't fall apart. Now widely available in cylinders to keep them moist, no picnic is complete without them, no mother would leave home without them.

So from the useless dry tissue has evolved the practical wet one. Let's hope that even now, paper scientists are working on a paper tissue into which you can blow your nose with absolute confidence. Then we can leave all those cold, wet noses to the dogs.

4

Girl Power

Men and women want the same things in life — a comfortable house, a good car, a haircut that doesn't make people point at us on the street. It's only the definition of those same things that varies. Women seem to think that guys have no taste. Well, if that's true how come we've come up with four perfectly good football codes in this country alone? Kick a footy to a woman and she'll try to découpage it.

If there is a fundamental difference between the sexes, apart from the obvious bits where one sticks out and the other doesn't, it's that women care about how things look, while men care about how things work. A woman cares about how she looks, but she also cares about how her man works. Men don't really care about how women work, as long as they look good. Confused? See you down the pub.

Sprung in spring

September sport spells domestic strife — and that's final!

September. Most will agree it's the start of spring. The sound of the start of spring is a point for debate, however. Europeans used to say it was the call of the first cuckoo. Some Australians think it's the cry of the first person to scream 'Ouch!' as a magpie pecks their head. But for ninety per cent of suburban males, it's the roar from neighbourhood televisions, all tuned to the same finals game. As the days get longer and warmer, the suburbs are alive with the sound of lawnmowers, whippersnippers, drills and saws — until the game starts. If you stand in your backyard as the TV coverage of that day's final begins, you can hear the hiss of beer cans being ring-pulled all over the neighbourhood.

It's hard for some women to appreciate this. All winter, the man in their life has been putting off vital maintenance work with the excuse that it's too cold or it's raining — he'll do it when the weather warms up. Now a warm, sunny weekend is stretching out before him and all he is prepared to do is be an armchair spectator while a lot of fit blokes in shorts hit each other at high speed.

September can be a time of disharmony as men and women fail yet again to understand each other. So let me answer some of your questions, girls.

Why don't you tape the game and watch it later?

A question asked by women in homes all over Australia on September weekends. Although the male of the species has a monopoly on the ability to set a video recorder, he chooses not to exercise this skill for finals games. This is because his mates will make it impossible not to find out the result before watching the tape.

Why can't you watch a taped game when you know the result?

A question sure to have men shaking their heads in pity. A match is only exciting if you don't know the outcome.

Why?

Good question. I don't know; it just is.

Why are you wearing your team's shirt and a scarf as you sit in your armchair, nursing a beer can?

Because men are boys at heart. They dream it's them out there, showing off their skills to the crowd. How we maintain this illusion is hard to explain, because not many professional footballers have beer bellies, a stubby in one hand and a remote in the other. Men have great imaginations.

Why can't you come to the garden centre? Didn't you watch the game yesterday?

That was Saturday's game, the preliminary semi-final. This is Sunday, the first elimination semi-final. There's more than one final, you know.

How can there be more than one final. Doesn't final mean last?

Not in football.

But your team didn't even make the finals, did they?

No, which is why we have to watch, so we can see how they went wrong.

I know some women are football fans too, and to

their husbands I can honestly say you're the luckiest men on earth. Unless your wife barracks for a different team. Now let's see how women respond to questions men have at this time of year.

Why do you resent me watching sport?
Because you watch it all. And you use 'the game' as an excuse not to do things.

I don't watch that much sport, do I?
Only the football, basketball, European soccer championships, Olympics, Wimbledon, motor racing, horse racing, golf ... and that's just the past three months. You think 'knit one, purl one' is a drawn soccer game.

Why do you want me to help you today?
Because it's a perfect day, the two of us could do the job in an hour and you could feel proud of yourself.

Why do you think I'm lazy just because I want to watch one game of football?
Because it's not just one game — couch potato.

Why don't you watch the game with me?
Because it bores me and I hate the way you explain all the moves. The same reasons you give for not coming to see romantic movies with me.

But why can't I cut the lawn next weekend?
Because the grass is a foot high and I think one of the kids is lost in it.

September can be a frustrating time for any of you wanting some action out of your man. But there are some pluses and you may find yourself celebrating during the finals, too. You can spend these weekend afternoons shopping with the other football widows. You can also expect impeccable behaviour from him until the end of the grand final. Grand final means the last final, the final final — the finale. And he'll agree to an expensive dinner out, a new lounge or a Bali holiday, anything — just stand in front of the telly and ask him while he's watching the game.

Not many footballers have beer bellies, a stubbie in one hand and a remote in the other

Lie back

We spent most of a recent Saturday buying a mattress. Talk about Goldilocks: 'This one's too soft, this one's too hard, this one's just right.' Then her voice pipes up from the other side of the mattress: 'It might be just right for you, but it's too hard for me.'

The salesperson hears the potential for a domestic drama. All her training comes to the fore; this is the chance to divide and conquer — and get a good commission. 'Do you know much about mattresses?' she asks innocently.

Now, unless you make mattresses for a living or have an unhealthy appetite for trivia, you don't know the first thing about them. 'It's part of a bed?' I respond confidently.

'Some people like the feel of a continuous coiled spring, others like independent springs. We have mattresses with continuous coils and large independent springs, and we have some with smaller, independent springs. Some have extra springs in the middle-third and there are several different edge-support systems. Do you know which you prefer?' We must have looked like a couple of stunned bunnies because the next thing we knew, we'd tested ten different mattresses.

There are two major problems with lying on a bed in a shop. One is that you're not in your natural bed state. You don't normally lie on your bed at home with your wallet and car keys sticking into you, your shoes on and a perfect stranger asking you how it feels.

The salesperson asked if partner disturbance was a major consideration. I didn't know what she meant. I hoped it meant that there is a mattress that eliminates snoring. But my previously undisturbed partner became obsessed with partner disturbance. 'Do that monster roll that nearly bounces me out of bed every night ... Go on, I've got to know if this mattress is better than the one at home.' I could see every man in the shop thinking, 'I've got to get out of here now before I look as stupid as he does.'

And then there's the choice. Choice is supposedly a good thing — it creates competition; market forces come into play, prices are kept competitive. It's the bedrock (sorry!) of capitalism. But by the time you've tried five mattresses, you have absolutely no idea how the first, second or third felt compared with the one you're lying on now. You might as well blindfold yourself, run around the shop and buy the mattress you fall on.

I found myself wishing I was in one of the old communist states, with a choice of People's Revolutionary Mattress Collective Type One or Type Two. Seems to me the only people who have an easy decision are those with back problems ... their mattresses have medical-sounding words in their descriptions, such as orthopaedic and chiropractic.

Healthy-backed people have to choose between Imperial, Plush, Super Plush, Mega Plush, Classic, Vintage — you'd think the inquiring minds that are always searching for the ideal combination of spring size and coil connection would have heard the words soft, medium and hard, wouldn't you? Any sort of grading system would do: springs per square metre, kilos per square metre, bounce-ability (measured in Elles). But no, they have to give mattresses names that describe them as accurately as those meaningless colour names. 'I'll have a Plush in Autumn Mist, to tone in with my Geelong Green bed linen.'

Eventually we bought the mattress of our dreams ... we hope. We are still waiting for it to be delivered. We think we both liked it, but there were several others which seemed pretty similar. It was almost certainly one of our ten favourites. There was a lot of partner disturbance on the night after our shopping trip. Every time I moved there was an accusation from the other side of the mattress. At three in the morning, she told me she was moving out and wanted to pack immediately. And apparently the base squeaks. The base didn't squeak last night, before we went shopping, but now the deal is done it allegedly squeaks. It seems we should have bought a new base as well. And somehow it was my fault; something to do with the monster roll.

Choosing a mattress is a very important decision. You'll probably spend a third of your time on it for the next ten years at least. But buying a mattress is almost as frustrating as deciding which spot to choose in an empty car park. Funnily enough, the solution is the same for both dilemmas — choose the one nearest the door to the shop.

Made to measure

Stature plays a large part in those kitchen and bathroom purchases

Size does matter. There, it's official. I'm talking about baths, but you knew that anyway. The thing is, when you're renovating, you have to shop for things that are normally taken for granted, like baths, toilets, everything including the kitchen sink. Which is how I found myself in a plumbing showroom, surrounded by strangers, sitting in a bath. Apparently everyone does it. Well, that's what my other half — taking into account the height difference, my other third — told me to get me in there in the first place. But if that's the case, how come I was the only one?

I wouldn't have minded, but she's the one who cares about the bath. For the amount I use the bath, it could be boarded over for six months of the year and used as a very small dance floor. I do shower every day, of course, but I'm getting to that.

You feel very self-conscious sitting in a public place, in a bath with your clothes on. Not as self-conscious as I'd have felt if I'd been nude ... plus I don't think the sales staff would have approved. It's hard to focus on the massage feature of the latest shower head when a naked man is sitting in a bath in the middle of the showroom. Although it would help to locate things: 'Yes, the vanity units are over there madam, behind the nude man in our Titanic Deluxe 1800 bathtub. No, that model doesn't have any handles ... Oh, love handles? Yes, he does, doesn't he?'

She was not content with making me try out this bath. I also had to lie down to see if it was comfortable. When you're 189 centimetres tall, no normal domestic bath is comfortable when you lie down. You have to rest your feet up over the end and look for all the world like a dying beetle. Of course, I lied. I assured her it was more comfy than the lounge — which is a two-seater, so I also have to dangle my legs off the end of that. I knew that anything less than total enthusiasm would mean she'd have me jumping in and out of baths all morning. Good practice for the next time I go bobsledding, but that will be about three weeks after the twelfth of never, so I've got plenty of time for that some other shopping day.

I did allow a feeling of satisfaction to creep over me when the bath lover tried out our new toilet for the first time after it was installed. She loved the design when she saw it in the showroom, even though there were many for half the price that I'd have been happy to sit on to read the paper. Still, I had agreed to the purchase with only three noises of disbelief, two comments about the need to win Lotto and one combined big shrug/sigh/shake of the head.

The loo is too tall for her little legs; she has to sit on it on tiptoe. 'You should have tried it out in the showroom,' I pointed out. 'Nothing to get embarrassed about, we all do it.' It is embarrassing, though, because people can't help but imagine how you'd really look sitting on the loo with your pants around your ankles. But at least they don't imagine you nude, like they do in the bath or shower. Oh yes, I had to get in the shower and simulate my cleansing routine to confirm there was adequate space. I thought it was a nice touch when she told me to pretend to drop the soap. The sales assistant was very amused and was insistent that I take his business card and phone him if I had any problems with the shower. Nice guy, but he kept winking at me. He should really get that looked at.

If you're part of a mismatched couple — I'm only talking about height here, a difference of thirty centimetres or a foot in old money — you'll know that eye levels vary a hell of a lot. It's important for things like mirrors, windows and any product with the words 'eye level' in its name — like oven grills. In a conspiracy of the vertically challenged, the kitchen supplier and the bath lover have set our state-of-the-art 'eye level' grill at my waist height. To see why the snags are on fire, I need to crouch, to bend over and peek in upside-down, or to dig a trench in that part of the kitchen. Then there's the risk of hot fat spitting at my sensitive trouser area. Clearly, the trench is the only answer.

I guess new appliances are like everything else in a relationship. You have to be prepared to compromise, to strike a middle ground where you're both equally unhappy. Either that or match up with a significant other who's the same height as you. As chat-up lines go, 'What height are you?' is a lot more original than 'Do you come here often?' or 'What's your sign?'

When you try out a loo, people can't help but imagine you on it with your pants around your ankles

Hell in high water

Real Aussie men don't have bubble baths!

It struck me the other day as I was lying in the bath. No, not lightning, a thought — the thought that men don't pamper themselves enough. Now then, girls, before you start pooh-poohing the very idea, take a moment to consider. Men are usually too impatient to run a bath, so it has to be a special occasion for us ... usually aching muscles from over-exertion. Even then we feel we're wasting time. We feel slightly embarrassed at putting some muscle soak in the water. Lying in the bath covered by all those bubbles, what if our mates could see us? We'd never live it down.

Now think about how women pamper themselves. The same bath that I lie soaking in would have scented oils. There might well be a couple of slices of cucumber over her tired eyes. Maybe the light would be off with a couple of candles burning to create a relaxing atmosphere. There'd probably be one of those waterproof cushions for her head to rest on. A guy walks in on this, he thinks — as well as his obvious wonder at how some things float and look better wet — that's nice, she's relaxing in the bath.

Okay, picture walking in on your man in the exact same position. You'd think how small and silly some things look when they float, and be convinced that he's having an affair. Either that, or he's getting too close to that mate of his who wears a belt that matches his shoes and knows a lot of show tunes. It's considered unmasculine for the Aussie male to pamper himself or care too much about his appearance. It's just not part of our culture. We all kid ourselves we've got the ANZAC spirit of resilience and fortitude. The diggers didn't complain about not having enough hot water to wash the conditioner out of their hair. Or getting a fingernail snagged on a barbed-wire fence. Or getting their hair wet when they were caught in the rain on the Kokoda Trail.

Hair is probably the defining difference between the sexes, even more than women's ability to bear children or men's ability to read a street directory. A man's haircut involves electric clippers, small-talk about footy and a meagre tip if, and only if, it looks like your mates won't fall about laughing at it when you go back to work. If a guy goes to a salon where they wash his hair first before cutting it, he's a bit of a dandy, he's got too much money or he plays in a band.

Now, women know how to pamper themselves at the hairdressers. They have to make an appointment! No wandering in on the off-chance on the way back from the sandwich bar. And each appointment takes, minimum, half a day. That's if it's going to be a hairdo that the man in her life will actually notice enough to pass comment on that same day.

This costs about the same as a full service, with new brake linings, brand-name plugs and an oil filter, for the average family car — and that's if you take it to the dealership and pay top dollar. Blokes cannot get a handle on the cost of women's hairdressing — these hairdresser people must earn what, twice as much as a heart surgeon?

I guess it's our own fault. Most men don't take that much pride in their hair. In fact, we're always sticking something on our head which has flattened our hair into a sweaty cow pat by the next time we take our cap off (usually the same day). And, obviously, we don't wear make-up. Well, not since the early eighties and the New Romantics, anyway. Not even if we're hideously pockmarked from an adolescence of mountainous volcanic pimples. To a man, the word 'foundation' means the thing walls are built on, not a peachy complexion.

Even using an aftershave is a stretch for most Aussie men. We might apply a tiny amount if we're feeling particularly refined. We certainly wouldn't do it to draw attention to ourselves. Not so, our American cousins; the average American male smells like the cosmetics counter at your nearest department store. I'm talking the average American male, like truck drivers, country-music fans, and disgruntled postal workers. The sophisticated American male is so perfumed that flies give him a wider berth than an overturned road-tanker full of tropical strength insect repellent.

I guess the Aussie male doesn't pamper himself too much because the Aussie female likes him that way. She doesn't want him to wax his back hair, file his fingernails or wear moisturiser. She loves his sandpaper chin, callused hands, broken fingernails, and smell of oil, sweat and overheated polyester. Don't tell us you'd have us any other way, girls, because you know what? We won't believe you.

Men are usually too impatient to run a bath; it has to be a special event for us

In and out of beds

Brace yourself men — it's that time of year again

The cooler months are upon us, and men everywhere are sleeping a little less easily in their beds. The women in our lives have got that look in their eyes. The look that always ends up with us getting sweaty and out of breath. It must be something to do with the longer nights but, certainly, their desire is higher. Yes, it's time to visit the garden centre again.

Autumn sends the female of the species into a frenzy of seasonal pruning and planting. And that means we lucky guys get to drive with them to the nursery. Next time you're there, take time to look around at the other couples. He'll be standing upright, with a faraway look in his eyes which he hopes won't be recognised as boredom. She'll be bobbing up and down beside him like a chook. She's smelling flowers, she's reading those little plastic labels in the pots, she's loading him up with pots like he's a pack mule.

Most of the time, we guys stand around doing difficult sums in our heads. Man A has a four-door sedan, Woman B has three large pots, five bags of compost, four bags of cow manure, three bags of tea-tree mulch, a ficus, a port wine magnolia, two camellias and a rain gauge. If Woman B loads all of her shopping into Man A's car, how long will it take Man A to walk home?

Garden centres are aphrodisiacs for women, and the owners know this. They also know that the word 'nursery' gets girls all gooey and cooey. So what do they call most garden centres? And whichever kind of nursery she's thinking about, it means work for us, whether it's decorating a room with cartoon characters or digging holes and filling them with compost. I try to understand what we're buying, but the more interested I sound, the deeper the hole I dig. If I ask where a certain plant is intended to go, I realise that I know nothing about my own backyard. She'll say something about it being for 'between the borus senselus and the watchya callems'.

It was a Swede named Linaeus who decided to classify plants by Latin names in the first place. By the time he got around to doing this, the last Latin-speakers, the Romans, had been gone for several hundred years. So you can blame the Romans for a lot of things — like using Christians as fast food for lions — but you can't blame them for all the fancy-pants Latin names. The point where you pass from being an enthusiastic amateur to full-on gardening tragic is when some of the Latin names get stuck in your mind. You find yourself looking at a wattle, but your mouth calls it an *Acacia howittii*.

Nurseries are pretty much like any other workplace. There are people who know a lot but don't want to share the information. There are the efficient types who will answer any question with yes or no so they can get back to work. And there are the know-alls. You can guess which one I always seem to pick. The know-all nursery person rattles off Latin names for everything including long-extinct ferns, rare species of spider, types of hoes and even cyclone fencing. He'll suck in the air through his teeth when you ask if a palm can survive in full sun. You'll say you want a red annual exotic, and he'll insist you want a blue perennial native. Try to buy as little from him as possible. I always carry an expired credit card to escape such situations. As a bonus, this embarrasses the hell out of your partner so you can't go back to that nursery for months.

For men, an increased interest in gardening is a sure sign of ageing. One day, at around thirty-five years of age, you finally decide to plant something. It withers and dies, and you discover soil needs fertiliser. You buy a bag of compost, flowers thrive and next spring you're buying red worms for your new compost bin, and making informed choices between tea-tree mulch and pine bark chippings. Water regularly, and there you are, a middle-aged gardener.

Who'd have thought that this would actually make you more attractive to your partner? Maybe that's why the first thing you learn when you're taught Latin, is *amo*, which means, 'I love'.

You can't blame the Romans for all the fancy Latin names for plants

Different strokes

Once we got a quote, all we had to do was decide on a colour

We've given the house a lick of paint for the summer. More than a lick, judging by the bill, and we hope it lasts longer than the summer, but you get my drift. The first thing we did was ask for a quotation. I don't mean the 'A horse, a horse, my kingdom for a horse' kind of quote, I mean a price from a painter. When we saw the costing, we held it up to the light, turned it around, looked at it in the mirror. It didn't matter which way we looked at it, this was a lot of money for painting a few windows, gutters and fascia boards. Our flabbers were well and truly ghasted.

I convinced myself, in fact both of us, that this was an aberration. I'd get another price and then we'd be in business. The second quote was higher. We decided to find a third painter and, you guessed it, the price was $1000 higher than the first. Several weeks passed and we decided to bite the bullet and go for the first painter. The number was unobtainable. He was no longer in the phone book, he'd gone bust. This really upset me. He must have been really cheap after all!

So we chose the second painter, and then all we had to do was decide on a colour scheme. This is the moment when you realise that the person you thought you knew and loved seems to see the world through kaleidoscopic glasses. It was obvious that the only way we could agree was to see a scheme we both liked. Every free moment for three weeks we were the strangers in the white car who stopped across your driveway and appeared to case your house for a burglary. It's a sad indictment of Neighbourhood Watch schemes that the police didn't question us once.

We decided on off-white and two shades of blue, which will probably look 'so nineties' in a few years' time, but fashion is everything, even in house colours. Now as you know, there are blues in many hues. This was when the painters rang to say they'd had a cancellation and could start the next day. You have to say yes, or you could go back to the end of the queue. It was too late to buy sample pots, so we made our colour selections from 35 × 70 millimetre colour swatches at sunset. The blues looked much lighter once they were on the house — funny that!

I was quite happy with both blues, thinking the front door was very cheerful indeed. When the allegedly tasteful one saw it, she screamed and told me I was going to have to paint over it. I'm sorry, but the words 'electric' and 'blue' go together in my book. She's getting used to it now, but every visitor has to fill out a questionnaire to gauge public opinion on whether it's stylish or daggy. I think it will go down to preferences, and if it goes against me I'll demand a recount and accuse her of vote-fixing.

All in all, it was a very painless process, except for the paint fumes, which had me writing some colourful prose for a few days. But a friend of ours had a very different experience. It appeared she had everything under control. She bought several sample pots and painted some stripes at the back of the house to see which she liked best. The more colours she tried, the less decided she became. If a concerned neighbour hadn't asked if she was going to paint her whole house in those stripes, she might still be deciding.

However, her mind made up she called in the painters. They told her they could start almost straight away, and asked what colours she wanted. She confidently sent them off with the names and numbers. 'Sample pot wasn't mixed properly.' 'Can't make that colour,' said the men in the overalls with paint all over them. She'd have to choose a more standard colour. She did. They went off again. Yes, they can get that colour ... in a month's time. Under extreme duress, she had to select her colours not from the colour swatches but from the tiny palettes inside a paint brochure.

And that wasn't the end of it. One of the painters was rather chubby. My friend had spent years nurturing a couple of garden beds in the front yard, but the overweight painter needed to get in past them to paint the bottom weatherboards. As our house-owner rushed to work, she left her teenage son with instructions to trim the edge of the bed about six inches or 150 millimetres, whichever system he felt more comfortable with. Eager to please Mum, he got hold of the whipper-snipper and took off a good half a metre. She came home, saw the carnage and cried.

I've heard of people being moved by a painter's work, but that's ridiculous!

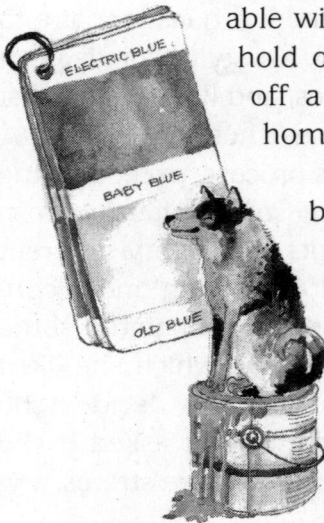

The words 'electric' and 'blue' go together in my book

Rug mugs

This country is in love with polished wooden floors

Timber floors are warm, welcoming and natural, yet classy. If they were people, they'd be Kerri-Anne Kennerley.

You do have to care for a timber floor, though. It can soon be damaged by gritty shoes and stiletto heels. Did you know that a stiletto heel puts a point load of about a quarter of a tonne on a floor? No? Well, I'm not sure if it's true myself, but it's not hard to believe when you see the pock-marks after your first floor-warming party. So when we moved into this place, with its hectares of polished timber floors, we knew exactly how to minimise wear and tear. We bought rugs.

Men will settle for any old rug — square, round, football-shaped — as long as it isn't pink. We don't care if it's wool or nylon — until we get static shocks touching a door handle. It can even have paws on four corners and an animal head at one end. But women demand more — it has to look good. And in her case, it has to be handmade and preferably Persian. So to the handmade carpet warehouse.

A handmade carpet is a thing of beauty, no doubt about it. The salesman tells us that the attraction of the handmade rug is that it has imperfections. In fact, if you believe everything the salesmen tell you, the more imperfect the rug is the better it is. They are like houses, they go up in value, he tells us. He shows us a threadbare, antique rug. Pre-loved. Secondhand — well, secondfoot really. He shows us the price tag. What I think must be the dimensions in millimetres is the price in dollars. Thousands. I look at my mat mate to see if she wants to run out of the warehouse too. She has one of those 'Wow, these must be lovely, look at the price' looks in her eyes. I feel that sinking sensation in the pit of my wallet.

We want three rugs, various sizes — two for the lounge-room and one for the hall. The hall runner we choose costs more than I thought we'd be up for to buy the lot. I've bought cars for less. If we are going to be up for this sort of money, I want to see every knot in every rug in the place. And I reckon we do. Men appear as if by magic to help turn back the piles of rugs one at a time so we can see the designs. The lower down the pile we get, the harder it gets for the men to turn back the rugs. And the more undecided we become. They get to the bottom of a pile of thirty or more when we decide on the third from the top. And we do it like this for three different-sized piles. We look again at the price tags and she looks questioningly at me. I see the flushed, expect-ant faces looking at me. They've shown us all their rugs. It's time for us to come to the party with the cash.

I need to buy time to think. We decide to go for a coffee to weigh up our options. The salesmen act non-chalant. They are confident that they have the finest of rugs that no sane person can resist. But not too confid-ent. We are sitting over our cappuccinos when we see one of them circling the mall to make sure we haven't gone. I know then that I have room to negotiate. A lot of us find haggling over a price annoying, time-wasting, embarrassing. I don't. I even got money off my lawn-mower because it was showroom stock.

The salesman sits at his desk and we sit so that he

has to move his head to look from one of us to the other. He writes the first offer down. Already discounted 15 per cent, he reckons. I shake my head with pity. Doesn't he think I know how to haggle? We hack off another 20 per cent. He doesn't flinch. Will we buy today? Cash? American Express, we reply. He isn't pleased. Cash is King. American Express is more like Princess Di. We are buying today. He wants us to be happy. Each carpet comes with a written certificate of authenticity. If we find we don't like them, he will happily buy them back. We think we have a good deal. We shake. He smiles. I know we've failed.

More salesmen carry our carpets to our car — they're smiling, too. If we'd haggled successfully, they'd scowl and we'd have to carry the carpets ourselves. 'What's up?' she asks as we sit in the car, nearly fainting at the camphor smell from the carpets. 'Got the rugs, didn't we?' But we didn't get the salesman's respect. She tells me I'm paranoid.

He hand-delivers the certificates a couple of weeks later. And tries to sell us another runner for the hall. 'You were right,' she says, 'he thinks we're mugs.'

A question of taste

Any change will trigger a huge chain reaction

It's a funny thing, this home ownership. Depending on how you look at it, it can be a source of great pride and joy or a total guilt trip.

Renting is so free of worries — you don't have to paint, even though you might want to, you can't renovate, even if you'd like to. Ultimately it's not your place to fix, you're only borrowing it. But when it's your own place ... changing one thing can trigger a chain reaction which leads to a complete renovation.

There's nothing which makes the difference between the sexes more apparent than talking about what should be done to improve the house. A woman thinks in practical terms such as a 'nice' bathroom and a 'decent' kitchen. A man tends to concentrate more on the finer things in life: a home cinema, stereo speakers in every room and three-phase power in the shed just in case he needs to run an industrial lathe. Agreeing about what needs doing to a house is something that's never going to happen and you might as well accept it. Let's take a simple example.

Most men don't really care what's in front of a window frame as long as there's glass in it. Tell us blinds and we think venetians. Okay, she says, get some quotes for some blinds, the sun coming through the kitchen window is so hot she can't do the washing up in the mornings. He thinks, better do it, or he may end up doing the washing up himself.

The blind man arrives. I'll rephrase that: the man selling blinds arrives and asks him what kind of blinds he was thinking about. He wasn't thinking about blinds at all — are there different types? Oh yes, says the blind man (the man selling ... you know). Venetians? The blind man then goes on to reveal that there are different widths of slat and different colours. He is amazed; who would have known? He makes executive decisions. Gloss, cream, 25-millimetre slats; she is going to be so happy with him when she gets home. What about the patio doors? The blind man says verticals; he sees the sense in that and makes more decisions on colour and fabric. She'll probably give him a cuddle for being this smart.

She comes home. He says, 'I got the quote.' She asks what sort of blinds. He says, 'Venetians.' She says they can't have venetians in the kitchen — too much steam and grease, they'll get discoloured in no time. Ahh, but they're gloss-finished, he points out. She's already onto the next problem. She hates verticals. He's all out of excuses. 'But they're cheap,' he says, hoping that will bring her round. Too late, he obviously doesn't ever listen to her, she doesn't know why she bothers. He is frustrated and goes off to play on his PlayStation.

Sound familiar? And that was just the margin of error possible on blinds for three windows. Imagine how far apart you can get on a whole extension. Men are broad-brush merchants, we think about the big picture; women are into detail, such as where to hang the little picture. A man can never ask too many stupid questions when he's trying to understand what his woman wants. She will say the word 'dishwasher' and know exactly what she means. She'll have in her mind the colour, the brand, where it should go in the kitchen and the type of powder she'll use. He'll think, does she mean like a machine or have we got to pay someone to come in and wash up? Even roof insulation can turn into a major debate. He finds out there are different types and gets quotes, but she wants to know what the difference is between wool, polyester and fibreglass. He says it's obvious, you wouldn't wear a fibreglass sweater, would you?

And the differences don't stop inside the house. There's the garden. You think you know someone until you start to garden with them. Guys think shed, garage, a few shrubs, bit of pine bark, some grass to mow, maybe a place to put an old car to do up. Girls think English cottage-style herb garden and vegie patch, place to grow flowers for cutting, roses, hydrangeas, marigolds, stone edging, no straight lines, nice and informal. The usual upshot is the man ends up mowing something shaped like the coastline of Norway and copping a serve every time he cuts up some of her daisy bushes which are now in the middle of his lawn.

Whatever you're about to embark on around the house, remember that men are from Wagga, women wish they weren't, and dishwashers are from the planet Zanussi.

The spring collection

Cleanliness is one thing, throwing things out is another

There's an English children's song which says that if you see only one magpie it means sorrow. In Australia at springtime, you know the reason for sorrow at seeing only one magpie is that its mate is probably swooping to peck the back of your head. Yes, it's that time of the year when people wear glasses on the backs of their heads to ward off magpies, the grass needs cutting regularly and some people like to spring-clean.

I like cleanliness as much as the next man. You're right, that's not saying much in most cases. But I really do like things to be clean. It's just that I can't actually throw things away. I'm a collector of my own personal memorabilia. About the only thing I can throw away without a pang of remorse is navel fluff.

The older I get, the worse it gets. A wise man said — or I may have seen it on telly — that a man knows he's getting old when he starts collecting old bent nails in jam jars. I have those jam jars — and plenty of empties ready for more nails, screws, nuts, bolts and washers. If it weren't for my mother, I'd still have all my childhood toys, model aeroplanes, books, cowboy hats, realistic-sounding machine guns and football programs. 'You never look at them anyway,' she said when I returned from university and went searching for my programs. I still get a bit teary when I think of all my memories of football games which have been lost. I've never under-stood her desire to be able to get from the door of my bedroom to the window without a machete and flame-thrower. Aren't mothers meant to keep our bedrooms as a sort of shrine when we leave home?

I've got old theatre programs, concert tickets, travel documents, all my old wage slips, cheque books — even I can't understand what I hope to achieve from hanging on to them. But I know that the minute I throw some-thing away, I'll want to look at it again. On the upside, I'm a model recycler. Things I would have thrown out — probably — I now get the chance to build into sizeable collections. Aluminium-can mountains, boxes of bottles, forests of newspapers and magazines. The feeling of pride when I put them out for collection isn't so much what I'm doing to reduce landfill, it's pride that I've actu-ally got rid of something.

I can imagine female readers finding this inexplic-able. Well, your equivalent is cuddly toys. These unlikely-looking imitations of wild animals, real and mythical, aren't given only bedroom space, but names. Women whom I regard as mature, sensible human beings have lime-green monkeys called Barry poking out of the tops of their beds. Now that's inexplicable! And don't get me started on shoes. I reckon ninety-nine per

cent of women in the world think Imelda Marcos was
just lucky to have so much storage space.

I don't think mixed marriages between hoarders and
other humans can work. We're passionate about what
we hoard. If our spouse throws one piece of memorabilia
away, the relationship is unlikely to survive. The resentment smoulders beneath the surface, emerging during
an argument months, even years, later. 'You threw out
Katie Kookaburra!' 'It was falling apart, it didn't have any
eyes and its insides were all over my pillow every night.
And while we're on the subject, where's my grand-final
program?' Tit-for-tat disposals can degenerate into *War
of the Roses*-style divorces.

There is a more civilised way to sort out such differences. You can arrange for professionals to come round
and have a sort-out for you. They ask if you really want
something, shame you into saying no, then throw it out.
I've got the number — I kept it because I knew it would
come in handy. It's in one of the piles of magazines in
the garage. You see? If I didn't hoard things, I wouldn't
have known where to start.

Resentment smoulders beneath the surface

5

Oh, The Humanity

Men are their own worst enemies. Or so people love to tell us. Clearly, this is untrue. Our worst enemy is the person that came up with that phrase.

If we're not our own worst enemies, there are enemies all around if you're prepared to put in the hard yards looking for them. The neighbour from hell is only a small step away for the average bloke with a short fuse and a fertile imagination.

People are out to get us. They don't accelerate away from us quickly enough when the traffic lights change. They phone us at all hours to sell us things by pretending to do market research. But it's not hopeless. You may already have won a major prize in the latest Reader's Digest Prize Draw.

Even our own bodies can rise up against us. The older they get, the more they want to disobey us and humiliate us. Of course, we could exercise more, but if God had meant us to exercise why did he let us invent the remote control?

Fat of the land

For most of us, summer is the time of reckoning

It's strange how you can convince yourself that you haven't gained weight until you put on your swimming togs for the first time every summer. They're your own little fat gauge. Generally, if you're a guy and you have to lean forward or look in a mirror to tie the drawstring, it's time to lose a few kilos. If you have a rippling six-pack above your drawstring, you can be very proud of yourself and be secure in the knowledge that women will admire your body at the beach and every guy will hate your guts — or lack thereof.

Our neighbourhood seems to be full of gut-busters. Guys and gals gamely strutting along, trying to look as though they're enjoying the walk. You just know they'd rather be at home with a pie and sauce. It's the price we have to pay for our lazy western lifestyle. We take the car for even the shortest of journeys. We use remote controls, food processors, dishwashers, electric can-openers and all other manner of electrical gizmos which save us time and energy and pile on the centimetres around our stomachs, thighs and bums.

Let's face it, a lot of us drive a car to the office, drive a desk all day, then drive home and slump exhausted into a chair, moaning about what a tough day we've had. If you both work, you may even be so tired with sitting down all day that you phone for a nice fatty pizza because you can't be bothered cooking. Shame on you. Order a deep-pan Supreme with extra anchovies and garlic, and I'll be over to help you with it later.

It's an easy trap to fall into but take heart, it's not your fault. We can blame the Americans. First they hit us with their fried chicken and special herbs and spices. Then it was their hamburgers and 'have a nice day'. Then all-you-can-eat family restaurants: clean, quick and cheap, and we can't get enough of it. They cash in on our tastebuds' love of saturated fats and our desire to order in rather than cook. To make this even more tempting, they produce lots of great television and then advertise pizza meal-deals during our favourite shows. This is the thanks we get for winning the war for them.

So how do we keep in shape with all this temptation? Sadly, it just means willpower. (Okay, I've just lost all the male readers.) The big causes of weight gain, apart from not walking anywhere near enough, are fats, sugar and alcohol. I've found that if you can be tough with yourself and eat fewer biscuits and chips and cut out the grog, the weight will actually go.

Yes, it is easier said than done. I don't think scientists spend enough time thinking about diet. The statistics show that an alarming number of us undertake diets every year, nearly all reverting immediately afterwards to their old bad habits. What we need is something to stop the cravings, like smokers have with nicotine patches.

Why not sugar patches, grog patches and fat patches? We're onto something here. It may be a while before science catches up, so experiment. Next time you have a sugar craving, tape a jellybean to your back. That way, if you are tempted to retrieve the bean and eat it, you'll think twice. I'm not saying it will stop your craving, but it will give you something else to think about ... like will it melt, will it stain and does very cherry flavour work better than the thrill of vanilla?

Alcohol can be avoided. You simply have to stop being sociable. People can't insist you have a drink if you're not there. And the words 'Drive in' at the local bottle shop are a suggestion, not a traffic sign. Fat can be avoided. Some avoid it too much, but let's leave Ally McBeal out of this. Fried foods are a lot easier to avoid in the hotter months. Salad is your friend, salad dressing isn't. And Caesar Salad isn't really a salad — it's just a very silly way to eat bacon and fried bread.

If you have to look in the mirror to tie the drawstring, it's time to lose a few kilos

Of course, the other option is to let it all hang out at the beach this year. There will always be someone there who looks worse in his or her togs than you do. Trouble is, the older you get, the fewer of them there are.

True grit

Brush-up on your dusting if you're renovating

By the time you read this, our builders will be gone. As renovations go, it was painless.

No flooded extensions, no electrical fires, no collapsing walls. But oh, the dust, the noise, the heat ... mainly, though, the dust.

Builders and dust go together like bacon and egg, or avocado and prawns. Except of course, you can see dust without seeing a builder. You can never have a builder without dust. You may not be able to see it straight away, but it's there. It's as if builders carry magic builder dust in their pockets wherever they go and sprinkle it around to make builder magic, like fairies sprinkle fairy dust. Except, where fairy dust makes all your dreams come true, a builder's dust makes all his dreams come true. Okay, you may be too old to believe in fairies, but you're not telling me you don't believe in builders.

When a builder starts work on your house, the dust never stops. It's everywhere, on every wardrobe, book-case and chair, all over dustsheets and yet all under them too. It somehow travels through the covers, through closed drawers and doors, and settles on clothes, books and CDs. If David Copperfield could do magic like that, he'd be famous. Even more famous. Okay, if you could do magic like that, you could be as famous as David Copperfield. Helps, too, if you've got a Dickens of a name, like Nicholas Nickleby, Oliver Twist or Little Nell.

Our builders were meticulously clean by industry standards. If the housing industry is thinking of creating a Special Award for Exceptional Clean-Up, our builders would win every year — a clean sweep in fact — broom broom. But there was still dust ... very fine dust, granted, but still there. In the first couple of weeks, we'd sweep the kitchen floor every night. The broom seemed perfectly efficient beforehand, but when used on builders' dust it was powerless — like an umbrella in a cyclone. The more we swept, the more dust seemed to appear, David-Copperfield-magic style but without the showmanship, the TV cameras or the teeth-whitening.

There were other unusual phenomena. It seems that builders have a dawn chorus, just like birds. Seven o'clock every morning, rain or shine, the builder has to communicate to other builders in the same neighbourhood with primitive banging and sawing noises. Immediately he comes into the house, he picks up a hammer, drill or power saw and makes as much noise with it as possible. Then, once he's announced his arrival to the whole world and made sure that all the non-builders are awake, he can settle down and have his smoko. For the rest of the day there'll be an occasional bang and the odd trip to hospital with a broken this or a bleeding that, but you won't hear the same sound level again until seven o'clock the next morning. Start with a bang, end with a whimper ... now David Copperfield wouldn't have built a career like that.

There are other little inconveniences too numerous to mention. Like if the missus is the type who doesn't like anyone to see her without make-up, except you and the beautician. Bumping into the workmen on her way to the bathroom before she has make-up on is traumatic. Standards have to be lowered, dressing-gowns found. Eye contact avoided. Mascara has to be applied in bed.

Preparing breakfast with the 'boys' around is a bit weird too, like being in a reality TV show. You're just living your life, yet you have an audience. They pretend not to watch you and you pretend not to watch them, but you can't help being aware of them. You have to be really nice to each other, so the builders think you're the perfect couple. You don't want it getting out that you're really like Bill and Hillary.

Yet, the strangest phenomenon of all is that we miss them when they're gone. Three months of our lives spent with increasingly familiar faces saying, 'G'day,' telling us what they did on the weekend and warming the toilet seat for us. And one day, they're not there any more. All that's left is our lovely new extension, a big hole in our bank balance ... and dust. Lots of it.

It's as if builders carry magic builder dust in their pockets and sprinkle it around like fairies sprinkle fairy dust

There goes the neighbourhood

Neighbours should be rarely seen and never heard

We have very good neighbours. Ah yes, but what makes a good neighbour? Someone who'll help you in a crisis — like clearing your blocked drains on a holiday weekend? Certainly. Someone who always greets you with a cheery 'How's it going?' on those rare moments you bump into each other out on the street? Probably. Someone who pops round uninvited to see what you're up to? Release the hounds!

I'm proud to be suburban and I like where I live at the moment — quiet retirees on both sides. Of course, they do have plenty of time to tend their immaculate gardens but if I don't look over the back fences I can avoid the guilt trip. It's with much trepidation, then, that we're thinking of embarking on the search for a new home. As Forrest Gump's mother might have said, home-buying's like a box of chocolates — you spend ages choosing but someone's always taken your favourite first. As for noise pollution — once you've made sure your dream home doesn't back onto the freeway or an airport runway, it's a lottery.

Sure, you can try checking your potential new home out at different times of the day. This will identify the most obvious problems — the neighbour who runs a timber-milling business in his backyard, the house with twelve kids, only one of whom is quiet and well behaved, the junk-yard dog retirement home three houses down. But all that can change in the time it takes you to move in and polish your floors. (And gee, doesn't that make some noise!)

I always found living in units to be hard, particularly if you have someone noisy overhead. The last unit I lived in during my single days had the noisiest, most eccentric man I've ever been forced to hide from in my life. Every time I ventured out he'd be lurking to tell me the latest wacky theory which had occurred to him at four in the morning when he was playing his Gambian hunting drums.

We lived on the ground floor of a duplex for a couple

of years. The people above were quiet enough, except when they expressed their love for each other, if you know what I mean. Also, unfortunately, the teenage son of the next-door neighbour kept his car in the front yard. He liked reggae music so much that he turned his car into one giant boom-box. Whenever he was short of petrol money, he would stay home, polishing his pride and joy with Bob Marley thumping out of the car's monster speakers, the bass turned up to 11, sending out shock waves which shook the paintings off our walls. I reckon all that vibration works its way out to sea and is the reason whales beach themselves — they want to get down to that reggae beat — man! It's as good a theory as any; ask a marine biologist.

I thought we'd found the ideal home a couple of moves ago. It was in a bushy cul-de-sac setting likely to make bushfire season seem more exciting than usual, and was apparently peaceful. It wasn't until we moved in that we realised just how many children lived next door — seven. They were actually very well behaved and only acted up when their mates came round.

But when they moved out, I was delighted to see a young couple move in. Okay, there'd probably be a baby crying in a couple of years, but it had to be quieter for a while. It was ... until they got the German shepherd. This beast could bark for Australia in the Olympics — and I'm talking the long-distance, marathon barking event. They didn't know he was a problem. When they were at home, their dog was happy and only barked if he was over-excited at feeling so loved and included. But when they went off to work every day, he barked at every movement until they came home again. This couple couldn't believe the dirty looks their new neighbours were giving them — particularly the bloke across the road who worked nights and was trying to sleep.

There's no doubt that noise pollution is one of the biggest stresses of city living. Readers living outside capital cities would be blissfully unaware that the people living under the airport flight paths make as much noise moaning about the jets as the planes make themselves.

I guess we all have to live and let live. If you want to be able to buy a litre of milk and a bag of chips at ten at night, you have to put up with the downside of city living. Anyway, I reckon the kid across the road who plays a drum kit in his garage is actually starting to get some rhythm. Fingers crossed he doesn't start a group, because if they're a Bob Marley tribute band, I'm out of here!

The late shift

Early birds catch worms, but they can keep them – give me a hash brown any day!

Daylight-saving is a rather strange term when you think about it. The Queensland government seems to regard it as some new-fangled thing that those southern try-hards do.

I believe the Queensland argument is built around the farmers' claims it upsets their cows' milking routine. This may be true, but tropical cows have much less variation in daylight hours than those in more temperate latitudes. A northern European cow still gives milk whether it basks in midnight sun in the twenty-four hours of summer daylight or stumbles around in the constant dark of a northern winter. Admit it, Queensland, you just like messing up our watches when we come up there for our holidays.

To the rest of us, daylight-saving means that we get our extra daylight hours at the end of the day, when they're of more use. We take the light from first thing in the morning, with its new-day chill and rudely awakening birdsong, and move it to the end of the day where we can take an evening constitutional and catch a nice romantic sunset with the love of our life. It makes our summer days seem longer and the season itself seems longer, too. I'd like it all year around, but the early morning Mafia would never let that happen.

Early morning Mafia? What's he on about? Simple: the world is run by early birds. They wrote the unwritten law (well, they talked about it over breakfast so that we owls missed the meeting). The law says that all noisy occupations must be started at 7.30 a.m. at the latest. If it needs jack-hammering, drilling or power-sawing, it must be done before I've woken up. I know the early bird catches the worm, but he's welcome to it. I'll stick with the lamb roast, thanks.

There's no doubt you're born a morning type, afternoon type or night type, but there are a lot more early risers than the other sort. It's probably the same ratio as right-handed people to left-handed. So if you're an early-morning left-hander, you're nowhere near as rare as a south-paw night owl. And if you're an afternoon ambidexter, you really do have the best of all worlds, don't you?

You can guess from this that I'm an owl. My father is up at sparrow's but I take after my mother. She's just about hitting her straps when my father goes to bed.

Cooking, sewing, decorating — it's not unusual to find her putting a final coat of paint on the ceiling at two in the morning. If the phone rings at 8.30 a.m., it means I have to wake up to answer it. The person at the other end is always amazed that I sound so groggy, and nine times out of ten they make comments like: 'Time you were up anyway, lazybones.' Of course, these same people don't get the joke if you phone them at eleven at night and give them a cheery: 'What are you doing in bed already, lazybones? The night is yet young.'

It's strange that our Anglo–Celtic society is so structured around what suits the early bird. You never see Late Bird Specials advertised, do you? Why shouldn't people who arrive after the morning rush hour get good deals on car parking too? Our cars are there the same amount of time and we don't cause traffic jams. Mediterranean countries are much more civilised, with their afternoon siestas and shops open well into the night, when you actually have the time to go shopping. But here, with the exception of Thursday nights — which are busier than Saturdays, so why bother — if you want to buy anything after six, you'd better hope it's in your local supermarket.

Maybe it has something to do with our war-loving ancestors. There were once just as many night people as morning people, but the morning people kept attacking at first light, thus wiping out whole generations of slumbering yet sophisticated evening-lovers. Those who were awake lived to fight another day, the sleeping didn't know if they were really dead or just having a very painful nightmare. If only night vision had been invented a few centuries earlier, office hours could now be 11 a.m. until 7 p.m.

I know I'm fortunate to have a career which lets me work the hours that suit me. It is now 12.02 a.m. and I feel more awake than I have all day. There's something about knowing most of the country is asleep (hello WA readers, how's your evening?) and you're still alert, wide-awake, making the most of the night. Maybe that's why the garbos like to empty the bins before everyone else is up. I know one thing for sure, though: I wake lots fewer people when I type on my computer than the bloke who empties those bins!

'What are you doing in bed, lazybones, the night is young?'

Sale of the century

Who in their right mind would move house?

Spring has sprung and we all know what that means. The azaleas are in bloom, magpies are dive-bombing anyone daring to go near their nests and 'For Sale' boards are springing up faster than weeds in your concrete path. Spring fever hits house-owners just like every other animal, except instead of an urge to find a mate and settle down somewhere a lot of house-owners have the urge to take their mate and settle down somewhere else. The warmer weather destroys our sense of reason. We actually set out to find some place to live that will cost us more money every month and into which our furniture may well not fit. It probably won't be decorated the way we like, either. House-owners just love making things hard for themselves.

Moving house is a huge decision, yet thousands of us do it every year. You need a pretty good reason to go through the hassle of tidying your house every week for viewings before the Saturday-morning frenzy of scouring the paper for properties to assess. Unless you need an extra bedroom, hate your neighbours or are on a witness protection program, you'd never go through such an upheaval.

It only takes a couple of weeks to acclimatise to the agent-speak in real-estate ads. 'Renovator's delight', 'cosy' and 'undercapitalised' are all code for don't look unless you're a builder and then only if you're a gambler too. 'Close to schools' means there's one across the street. 'Bus stop nearby' means that the No. 38 turns around in the driveway twenty times a day. 'Convenient for all transport' means the house is in a cul-de-sac between a six-lane freeway and the railway line, and directly under the airport flight path. So once you've cracked the code and whittled the ads down to possibles, you have to get out the street directory. This usually allows you to cut the number of properties in half as you identify those which are on busy roads, next to an abattoir or on a one-way street accessible only by ferry.

It's then that the first law of house-hunting kicks in. The two places that seem most suitable are twelve kilometres apart and have quarter-of-an-hour viewings at exactly the same time. Even if you're lucky enough to have two cars, don't even think of splitting up and doing one each. You do not know what your partner is looking for even if you've been together for twenty-five years. Try this simple test. Does your partner like a full-sized bath? A wall oven or conventional stove? Single or double garage? Mock-Tudor letterbox or oil drum on a stick? Trust me, you have as much idea of the details that your other half is looking for in your new home as you do of what moon dust tastes like.

It's hard to be sensitive to others' feelings when you're house-hunting. You're on a schedule and you're on a budget. You need to look, decide if the place has what you want and, if it hasn't, whether you can afford to put it in. All this needs to be done in about two and a half minutes if you're going to make it to the next viewing. It's the biggest investment of your life and you spend less time deciding on it than buying a new sweatshirt.

If you're selling your home, never be around for the viewing. It's hard not to feel insulted when someone marches into the home you've lived in and loved for years, looks round for ten seconds, and says something like 'Way too small, this won't do' and walks straight out again. You want to run after them and explain what a great place it is, to regain your self-respect and justify your lifestyle. No, best not to be around for that, unless you have a really strong ego or a fully loaded super-soaker for instant revenge.

Of course, if you're buying, you're excused any insensitivity. You can walk into a stranger's house and say pretty much the first thing that comes into your head. 'People actually live here?!!!' You can laugh out loud at their choice of curtains. You can say things like 'Phew, it stinks!' and chances are that nobody will be offended — unless the real-estate agent has an underarm freshness problem. Of course, it's best to check there's no one standing nearby with a super-soaker. Believe it or not, you're not the only one reading this.

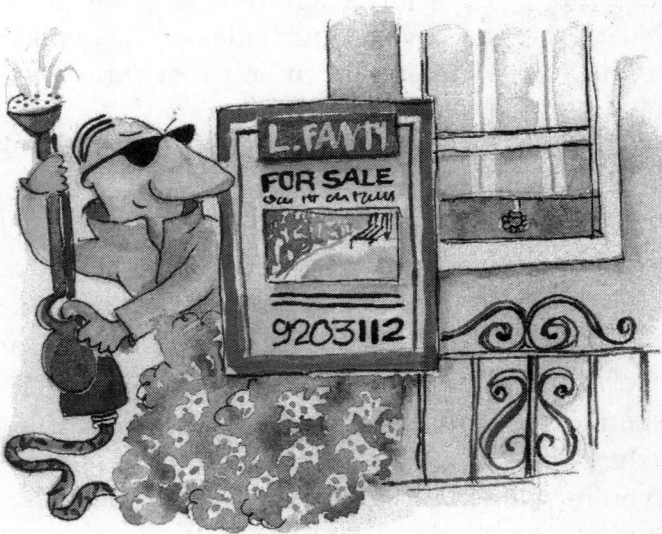

Check the owner's not standing by with a fully loaded super-soaker

6

When Furniture Attacks

There are people who believe that inanimate objects are alive. Anyone who's spent an afternoon with a self-assembly bookcase knows that they're right. Then there are the people who believe in karma. They think that what you do to others will eventually happen to you. Funny, I don't remember ever breaking the ignition coil, air-conditioning condenser and fuel pump in the same week on anyone else's car.

Some people spend their lives trying to find meaning in things that don't work out for them. I mean, apart from the GST. Sometimes, though, you've got to face facts, stuff just happens. The lesson to be learned is to deal with it like a mature adult — like that's any fun.

One bin behind

Miss bin night once and you're in real trouble

We've been having a bit of a clean-out. As usual I've fought hard to keep everything but I've had to make concessions. Old magazines had to go after I admitted under interrogation that I probably wouldn't ever read them again. I didn't give in on the footy programs, though; they provide me with a memory of where I was and who I was watching on a given winter weekend. Very good cure for long-term footy memory loss, is a *Football Record*.

We've also thrown out a lot of old cardboard boxes. You know, the ones for the stereo and video that you keep to pack them back in when you move because you don't trust the removalists. Well, we've decided that by the time we move again none of that stuff will be worth enough to worry about. Suddenly we have cupboard space. I felt very public-spirited putting the cardboard out on the nature strip for recycling. But there's a problem. I've now got a bin bag full of polystyrene packaging. And that's just the start of it.

We went to Uluru and the Olgas for a week. That wasn't the problem — they're very nice big rocks indeed and would take pride of place in anyone's backyard. (I'd fix up a few floodlights if they were mine, but they're not.) Judging from the tourists, the Yanks, Japanese and Poms would be only too happy to have them in their country. But let's face it, we have the best setting. Anyhow, the problem. We had a house-sitter. Don't get me wrong, she wasn't the problem either. She did a fine job as always — she kept the cat alive and didn't burn the house down, and that's gold-medal-winning house-sitting in my book. But, while we were away, the house was lashed by a night of Old Testament-style weather. You know the sort of thing — horizontal rain, thunder, a plague of frogs. This night happened to be bin night so, perfectly understandably, our sitter forgot the bin.

That's the problem. We're a bin behind. If it's never happened to you, then I hope it never does. If it has, you know what I'm going through right now. Being a bin behind wouldn't have mattered in the old days when we had huge bins for all our garbage. But in these righteous recycling times we compost, we bundle papers, we put out glass and aluminium separately, and the huge bin is solely for garden rubbish. Put anything other than garden rubbish in that bin and it will be ignored at the next collection. (At least they don't tip it all out over the nature strip as they did in the good old days.)

So in these enlightened, eco-friendly times, if we miss just one collection, the garbage bin is full from there on. No room in the bin, whoever you are. You're going to have a spare bin full of full garbage bags until you die.

I don't know what to do. It's been three weeks. The bin goes out on Wednesday night, I fill it immediately it's emptied on Thursday morning and then I've got another bin full of bags ready to go in by the next Wednesday. You can't leave out bags on their own; our council won't collect them. That's because the council no longer employs the team of whistling, cheerful, smelly garbos to rattle and yell and spill your bins on the road, does it? No, your rates pay for the truck and one driver. Our driver is a woman! And there's a look in her eyes that says: 'Someone burned her bra so I could do this. I'm grateful, really I am. I just wish the overalls had some pleats.'

I'm getting desperate. But I don't want to get caught out by one of my neighbours as I loiter by his bin late on a Wednesday night, sneaking a look inside to see if there's room for one of my bags. Anyway, wouldn't it be illegal, garbage fraud or something?

I really don't know what I'll do. Eat out for a week

maybe. We could break down the bag full of polystyrene beads and make a beanbag, I suppose. At least we could throw that out on the next council clean-up day. Of course, I could always try the next street. They don't know me.

So be very afraid: next time you go to bring in your empty bin it could be full. And you'll hear me laughing from blocks away.

I don't want to get caught by a neighbour as I loiter by his bin

Going nuts

You need to check the parts before assembly

We bought some safari chairs to sit on for a bit of comfort around the plastic patio table. A safari chair is a lot like a director's chair — in fact, it would be the chair a director takes on safari. But the point is, we arrived home with the two chairs nicely packaged in a couple of flat(ish) packs. I opened them to find instructions, a few wingnuts and the fabric for the seats loose in the ever-present clear plastic bag. I felt cheated. The words weren't there on the box. You know those words, the catchphrase words that symbolised the get-the-furniture-home-quickly-in-as-many-pieces-as-it-takes nineties: 'Some assembly required'.

You probably think this should be no problem. After all, don't I usually advocate doing it yourself? Well, yes. But you can only do it yourself in materials that you can work with. The thing about the chipboard-based modern furniture is that if you do try and work with it using ordinary tools, you tend to be left with a pile of wood chips and bent laminate.

They pre-drill their furniture in the factory because they know how to do it, and they ain't telling us. So it's not do-it-yourself. Somebody else has already done it. It's doing what somebody else has already done. Self-re-assembly. But even so, men thrive on demonstrating their greater spatial awareness in three dimensions and their ability to decipher an instruction sheet. Don't they?

You still don't understand. There's no challenge, unless you strike lucky and get something from one of the new Asian boom economies, where everything is lost in the translation. When you don't have ABC in your alphabet and the person translating is a backpacker trying to earn enough for his plane fare home, step-by-step instructions become one step forward, three back and two to the side. That's when self-assembly furniture is fun!

I blame the Europeans. They made self-assembly compulsory for their furniture. They couldn't have done it without that bloke Allen. You know, the inventor of the Allen key. And just to turn the last chipboard screw with

the plastic dome insert in the coffin of ready-made furniture, they came up with cute names for cupboards,
wardrobes and even bookcases. 'Have you met Bjorn?
That's him there with the books. Next to Vince, the magazine rack!'

Now don't get me wrong. They make good products,
and at affordable prices. I'll rephrase that, you make
their good products. Any book looks good in a Bjorn. It's
just that it seems wherever you shop now, instead of the
old six-to-eight-week wait, you buy the furniture, put it in
the car and, provided all the parts are there, assemble it
by tea-time. Fair enough in the case of something bulky.
But safari chairs? Surely something which folds up to
stack away can be put in a box in one piece?

Machines can do everything except actually put the
stuff together. So the furniture manufacturers include us
in their workforce. You, brothers and sisters, are unpaid
labour for giant multinational sofa-bed and side-table
conglomerates. People on the other side of the world are
growing rich on the fruits of your labour. As I look
around my SOHO (trendy term for Small Office, Home
Office — actually it's one of our bedrooms full of computers and stuff), I realise that I assembled the desk this
computer sits on, the hutch the printer is on, the fax
machine table and even had to put the back on the chair
I'm sitting in. How does anybody ever get their own
work done when we're spending all our time doing it for
furniture companies?

Won't be long before computer companies cotton on
and we're putting in motherboards and hard disks ourselves. With Allen keys. It's the thin end of the wedge.
We've got to put a stop to it now or nothing will come to
you as a finished item.

This book comes to you via Ralph, an IBM 386SX clone and Huey, his mate the inkjet printer. Some assembly required. Here's the last sentence. Nreitelghronere ioinre ??/ !! —-,... 4. Please follow the instructions on page 864 carefully.

Everyone makes mistakes

Being a humble consumer isn't easy at times

Everyone makes mistakes — even me. It's one of life's truisms, because without making mistakes we couldn't learn from them and we wouldn't be the well-rounded interesting people that all my readers undoubtedly are.

I once made one of those embarrassing mistakes it takes years to own up to — eight to be exact. It was a steamy Sydney summer and wandering round a department store I saw an evaporative/cooler fan. It looked the bee's knees and as mortgage rates were about eighteen per cent back then, I couldn't afford a real air-conditioner — I could barely afford to put water in the ice trays. In the cool air-conditioned comfort of the shop, it was easy to imagine that this impressive-looking fan could make our sweatbox of a house livable. But as my well-worn Visa number was being checked by phone — remember that? — not for a moment did any logical thought enter my head. This is nothing unusual for me at any time of the day actually, but that's no excuse.

Those in the northern states will know my mistake. For an evaporative cooler to work, the water has to evaporate. Without getting too technical and boring you with dew-point temperatures, saturated air, and why we say 'Hailstones as big as golfballs' and not 'Golfballs as big as hailstones', Sydney in February has about one hundred per cent humidity about one hundred per cent of the time. In other words, steam heat. In simple terms, there's no 'dry' air for the water to evaporate into. So my new fan didn't cool at all, it just pushed damp air at me, a couple of degrees cooler than the hot damp air I was already sitting in. But you live with mistakes like that because it was too embarrassing to go back to the shop and admit that you were asleep during all the geography lessons on meteorology. The fan also had a heating element supposedly to keep you warm in winter. Maybe it would have ... if you lived in Darwin. I put it down to experience, I put it under the house and I put it out on the kerb a respectable two years later for a council clean-up.

In these days of low mortgage rates and low inflation, there's so much more available money to make stupid purchases. Last winter, on the first cold day, we and many others arrived at a well-known gas and wood-fired heater specialist. Three winters of shivering were enough — we needed a gas-fired, fan-assisted heater and we signed up there and then. 'Does it come with remote control?' we asked, as we only have about eight zappers in the lounge-room at the moment and you can never have enough technology. The saleslady seemed a tad puzzled and didn't have one around to show us, but said yes and allowed for it in the price. A few weeks later, the builder was installing the heater and said that he'd put in a wall switch as well as the remote control we'd ordered. He asked if we were sure we needed the remote control; going without it could save us about two hundred bucks. I said we definitely needed the remote. It didn't even click when he gave one of those 'Suit yourself' shrugs.

On completing the installation of the heater, the surround and all the stuff to make it burn and fan, he handed me the control. If it had been an old cartoon, I'd have grown a couple of long ears, a horse's head and a sign reading 'Jackass' would have appeared around my neck. Now you'd think a remote control for a variable-speed, fan-assisted heater would operate say, the temperature setting and the speed of the fan. No. On and Off. Just the two buttons: On and Off. No wonder the woman in the shop had looked at us as if we'd each got three ears and green hair — my hair was actually a bit green due to a freak lawnmowing incident...

I've made so many unwise purchases. My latest little gem was something stupid for the garden. It's said you can't con an honest man — well, you can easily con a lazy one. I was cruising the aisles of my local hardware store on my daily check for new gadgetry when I spotted it. A solar-powered garden light. It cost as much as a box with half a dozen conventional low-voltage lamps, but I wouldn't have to wire it in, I could just stick it anywhere and hey presto, sun goes down, light comes on, garden looks a million bucks. Technology at its finest. If only the instruction booklet had been on the outside of the box.

To get the best effect, the thing has to be in full sun. And if it isn't, it doesn't stay lit for very long. In fact, after a cloudy day a better description would be a solar-powered garden dark. And it only has a four-watt globe, which means I can just about see the bottom two leaves of any plant nearby and none at all if I'm a couple of metres away. Another mistake, but I am learning, I promise. I know that one day I'll see the light — if I can just find the place in the yard which gets full sun.

Going down

Don't ask me to chair a meeting — it'll end in tears

I feel we know enough about each other now for me to reveal a secret known only by a few of my closest friends. Over the years, I've written about many of the intimate details of my life in an effort to keep the page on which my column occurs free of advertising. All I know about you is that sometimes some of you write or telephone me to say nice things. So far nobody has sent money, but even so I'm prepared to really open up and confess — I'm a chair-breaker.

I've never intentionally tried to give you the impression that I'm a skinny bloke, but I've never compared myself with Homer Simpson either. It's not that I'm particularly fat or heavy — although, to keep that in perspective, I think Mike Tyson's fighting weight is only a shade over my walking weight. But put me in a certain kind of chair and it's only a matter of time before one of us cracks. Up to now, it's always been the chair. And I'm sure my reaction is a lot less dangerous than Iron Mike's would be. You have my assurance that, however spectacular my fall, everyone's ears will remain intact.

The first time I encountered the problem was a few years back when I was sitting in a director's chair on a friend's balcony. Fortunately, I didn't have my back to the seventh-floor view, because as I reached forward for a peanut or a chip — the memory's a bit hazy about which — there was a ripping sound and I was catapulted backwards. I knew the chair must have collapsed, but didn't know if the ripping sound coincided with a new opening in my shorts. In fact, the chair seat had torn in two and my shorts were intact — not the worst result possible. Of course, the laughter and accusations implied that it was in some way my fault. 'Lard-arse', I believe, was one theory. But my inspection of the seat fabric revealed years of neglect. Salt-water corrosion and sun damage had made the chair an accident waiting to happen. They can think themselves lucky I didn't sue.

Now, I like to make people laugh, but not by falling over, off or under things. And there's nothing more annoying than people guffawing with laughter just because you're no longer sitting in front of them. I mean, why is that funny? Of course, they make concerned noises about your health, but this is usually after everyone has had a good laugh and a few puns have been tossed around, 'Three chairs for Steve!'

Last Christmas Day was the most recent demolition of some friends' furniture. It looked solid as a rock, a stylish, all-timber folding chair. Imagine my surprise when I leaned forward for my severalth oyster and found myself heading backwards onto the lawn. The timber had rotted through and the whole back of the chair had snapped off. 'Had a bit too much Christmas chair,' somebody said. Oh, how I laughed.

I'm just as destructive with our own chairs, which I always try to repair and which always break when I'm testing them. Believe me, most of those supposedly invincible adhesives are unsuitable for fixing chairs. So far, the count is one director's chair, one safari chair and one dining chair. The only one that was repairable was the dining chair, not that I sit on it. That's the generous kind of guy I am, prepared to let someone else get the laughs for a change.

The common factor seems to be that the chair breaks either when I'm leaning forward or when I'm getting up. Now to explain this is a bit tricky, but it's all to do with moments. Structural engineers will know what I'm getting at. When I'm sitting, my back is reasonably perpendicular to the seat and, therefore, to the ground below. But when I lean forward, that part of my weight is trying to push my whole body backwards,

Jail breaker

with only the chair providing the resistance. Or in my case, often not providing enough resistance to stay in one piece. It's like why you should climb over a gate at the hinge and not at the catch ... only it's not really. You see, I'm completely blameless. Now, if only our schoolteachers had explained vectors by describing people reaching for oysters while seated in a director's chair, I'm

Ice breaker

sure we'd all have achieved better grades.

So there you have it. Ask me at your own risk if I'd like to sit down. And always give outdoor furniture the once-over before sitting down. Remember the eighth rule of comedy: it's always funny when someone falls out of a chair — unless

Chair breaker that someone is you.

Labours of love

Are you prepared to accept the renovation challenge?

We had overnight guests the other night. They'd taken on the task of sanding and polishing the timber floors in their inner-city terrace. Carpet-layers must be doing it tough — it seems half the country now has polished floorboards, while the other half makes do with the wall-to-wall, beige berber twist-pile that's been there since the seventies. The only new fitted carpet I've seen of late is in photographs for the Gold Coast homes offered in sweepstakes draws — strangely it always seems to be brand new beige-berber.

Anyway, we offered our friends a room for the night, as their plan was to put a coat of sealer down last thing Saturday afternoon. The fumes would be pretty hard to take and they jumped at the chance not to inhale for a night. It was only between the barbecued octopus and the char-grilled atlantic salmon cutlets — sophisticated barbecue chef, eh?! — that we discovered why they were so grateful.

It seems that to polish their floors they'd had to pile all their lounge-room furniture into their eat-in kitchen. By the time they had five bookshelves, two lounges, coffee table, dining table, chairs, television, hi-fi and sundry lounge-dining bric-à-brac in the kitchen (they wisely sent their large golden retriever on holiday), they were left with a twisted corridor to the backyard the width of a slim person turned sideways. They reckoned if their feet had been any bigger they couldn't have got through. The previous night, they'd finished a coat of sealer at about eight in the evening, then had to squeeze through into the backyard. There they played cards till two in the morning waiting for the floor to be dry enough to walk on, so they could reach their bedroom. Well, they didn't really play cards all the time. The cards became too soggy in the rain to shuffle and the print was coming off so their best hands were actually on their hands.

Some friends of ours have broken up, citing renovation as grounds for divorce. Seems the main grounds for divorce are now (starting with most common): infidelity, renovating, irreconcilable differences of a non-renovating nature, or desertion to go fishing/ to the footy/ to the cricket/ to the pub/ to live in the shed.

When a couple sets out together on a life of renovating, they have to be compatible. We know one couple who now live in a renovated house where no detail is left undone, including skirting outlets for connecting speakers to the home-entertainment surround-sound system. We knew the relationship would survive, but the time scale they imagined was always going to be too short for such a pair of perfectionists. Come midwinter they were in a state of constant retreat from the builder's forces. There were workmen in the lounge-room, in the kitchen, in the hall, in the bathroom, in the roof. At first light, the new attacks came in waves: plumber, renderers, roof tilers, wall tilers, electrician. The noise was unbearable, with radios blaring, mobile phones ringing, endless tuneless whistling — even the occasional sound of hammering and drilling.

Finally, on a cold, starlit night they made an escape and came round for dinner. Their house had temporary electricity, but only enough for lighting. They sat in front of our gas heater, the stereo playing in our carefully mood-lit lounge, like refugees from a small communist country where they had to queue for three days to buy a slice of bread and a lump of coal.

Their finished house is a sight to behold. And you can compare it with the old, because being true renovators they have more before and after photos than a weight-watching advertisement. And there's no faster way to weight loss than doing your own renovating. I once worked with a bloke who'd just bought a new house and was renovating it in the evenings. He was putting new holes in his belt within a fortnight. After a month, we were all seriously concerned he might slip through the gaps between the floorboards — and they were tongue-and-groove!

They were in a state of constant retreat from the builders

7

Fur, Feathers and the Backyard Jungle

Generally we like animals. Not enough to stop most of us eating meat, even though we can easily make the mental link between a fluffy little lamb and the Sunday roast. If you're going to reincarnate as an animal, though, be a pet. You won't get fattened up as much, you might be dressed up in human clothes and pulled around in an old pram by the kids, but when the end comes you won't end up in a pie.

Don't tell me that we're higher up the evolutionary chain than pets. Talk about a free ride. They don't pay rent, we feed them every time they whinge at us, and as for dog-owners with their little scoopers and plastic bags...

The cat's whiskers

One could assume that cats are the superior life form

There's no doubt cats have got it made. Humans feed them, then go off to work every day so they can afford the house and garden for the cats to laze around in the lap of luxury. The thing that sets cat people apart from say, dog-owners, is that cats choose us. If a cat doesn't like you, he moves next door. Or two houses down. Or, if he really dislikes you, goes feral. So cat people have a perpetual need to prove to their cats that they are worth living with. That's why we believe that we're such nice people — our cats give us daily tests to prove it.

Pet-food companies want cats' approval just as much as we do and are all vying for their wholesome meaty chunk of the action. Small foil containers with elegant names and extravagant contents. Cats love them. But there's a sting in the tail; the next time you give them 'normal' tinned food they look at you as though you're trying to feed them dog meat — the ultimate insult to a cat. My cat loves the current trend for 'casseroles' and 'chunks in jelly'. He also likes those Devon-type sausages in different flavours. In fact, if there were a sausage made of jelly in gravy, it would be all he'd eat. I wonder if I'm killing him with kindness. Is it the equivalent of feeding him hamburgers and chips?

The vet gave me some 'Professional Cat Food' to try (on my cat). Now this is brilliant marketing. It really appeals to a cat's sense of superiority. He's a professional cat, he thinks. This is what he should be eating, because he's not just any old moggy, he's a professional. And how about a tablecloth and a linen napkin for good measure?

There are many other feline home comforts, such as cat flaps — magnet-operated for the cat who likes security — cat baskets and the humble, yet vital, litter tray. You can buy him cat litter made of recycled phone books; soft, strong and in two colours — off-white or off-yellow. That's what the Telstra book muncher does — you give him your phone book, he munches it into cat litter, and you buy it back. No wonder Telstra is so attractive to investors. But I do think cat litter made from recycled phone books is a sound idea. It's comforting to know that if your cat were ever unable to get to his tray he could make alternative arrangements in the Yellow Pages.

But it's not easy to impress your cat, is it? You can spend a small fortune on a sophisticated array of gizmos and still be left with the impression that Puss thinks you're a bit of a try-hard dummy.

On the home-entertainment front there are toys. Usually the toy resembles a mouse and has a bell on it. This sort of stereotypical thinking is very insulting to a cat who understandably thinks that your total level of understanding of him dervies from Tom and Jerry cartoons. Then there are the miniature carpet-covered objects and pretend trees. These are supposed to stop Kitty plucking the arms of your new lounge — the trouble is, they don't make any in a full-sized lounge shape that your cat really would enjoy scratching. So you arrive home from the pet shop with a box full of toys, the climbing tree and scratching post. And your cat loves them. He loves them because it's his chance to show that he can't be bought with money. They love playing mind games with us. Their usual reaction is a curious couple of sniffs, a yawn and then either a return to sleep or a saunter to the food bowl. What your cat won't do is play, climb or scratch what you've just bought in the vain hope of receiving some gratitude.

Whatever you do, don't demean yourself any further. There's nothing more pathetic in a cat's eyes than to see a grown human being down on his or her knees, patting at a plastic mouse with a hand clenched like a cat's paw. Or pretending to scratch a carpet-covered witch's hat. Your cat knows this isn't what you usually do. And it doesn't relate the sad image back to its own graceful feline actions. He's not refusing to copy you because he's stupid, you're stupid to think he'd be so undignified. If your cat wants to humiliate you further, he might sit in the box or play with a piece of the packaging from the toys, to show he can make his own entertainment, thank you very much.

I make my cat wear a collar with a bell — to protect native wildlife. That's my excuse anyway. Actually, it's my revenge. I know he finds it humiliating. Now he knows how I feel when I'm cleaning his bowl, washing his blanket or playing with Mr Mouse — last year's Christmas present — which I tied to the Hills Hoist.

You're left with the impression Puss thinks you're a bit of a try-hard dummy

Dog of a decision

We're seriously thinking about getting a dog. And you do need to think seriously about it; dogs need a lot of attention. You have to give them as much thought as you do to having kids. And you have to pay for a dog — they don't just happen after one too many drinks on a Friday night.

For a start, the cat's not going to like it. He doesn't even like other cats. And he's been an only cat for years now. I wonder if he'll be smart enough to deal with it. He really isn't so bright. I've had cats who can open doors by hanging on the handle, and one who could lie on his back and pummel the edge of a biscuit-tin lid with his paws to get at the dry cat food I kept inside. About the smartest thing this cat does is steal things out of the bin (I feel quite proud of him for having the initiative), but he normally steals something he doesn't eat, such as pizza. And he might get jealous of a puppy ... you don't have to be clever to be jealous, do you?

The other thing is what kind of dog to buy. I'm a Border Collie man myself. I don't mean that I'm some hideous mutant, half-man, half-sheep dog, like something out of a Greek myth. I mean I like Border Collies; they're so intelligent. There, you've got it straight away — I want a clever dog, yet I'm happy with a cat which scratches to be let in at one door to the lounge-room when the other one is wide open. It doesn't make sense.

And it doesn't make sense having a Border Collie if you don't have a farm or a spare twenty-three hours a day to exercise it.

She, the cat's adopted mother, grew up with a Westie. No, not someone from the western suburbs. I mean a

West Highland White Terrier, like Wee Jock in *Hamish Macbeth*, the TV series set in Scotland. She loves Westies not because they're intelligent — because they're not — but because they make her laugh. And I admit there is something about the perky-eared, stumpy little fellas that makes me chuckle.

But I don't know what Westies are like as pups. Collies are pretty destructive, but it's mainly out of the house. They're a gardening sort of pup, the kind of dog which likes to replant various species of shrub — but only after a good shake and pruning with the puppy teeth. And they always dig the hole way too deep. I'd know what to expect with a Collie — if you invite more than three people to a barbie, the dog will try to round them up and keep them in one corner of the garden. But terriers aren't sheepdogs, they're ... well, they're terriers. So once they start something they don't stop. Like unravelling nearly priceless Persian rugs. Like eating shoes until all that's left is the little metal bits the laces go through. Like tearing at the edge of the lounge until it looks like a half-sheared sheep.

And then there's the walking. Collies are good on a leash because they're easy to train. But what if Westies do not even understand that walks are a good thing? I might be out there in full view of the neighbours, pulling this small, white puppy along the nature strip on its backside because it thinks 'Walkies!' means 'Sit!' Anyway, a dog with little legs like that can't walk very far, surely. I'm going to end up taking him for a walk and carrying him home because a stroll to the shops for a six-footer like me will be a half-marathon to him. And how silly am I going to look?

I don't know how sniffy Westies are. You know what

I mean; you take them for walk and they stop and sniff at every blade of grass, telegraph pole, car tyre, kerb, postbox, your leg — you've been out half an hour before you've even got past your next-door neighbour's driveway.

And there's the never-ending leg-lifting. Some dogs seem to make one bowl of water go a very long way. And the inevitable confrontations; a Westie would probably fight other dogs head-on. Collies don't, they're sneaky. The other dog marches by thinking the Collie's a wimp, then next thing the Collie bites his ankles. But terriers take on dogs ten times their size. They don't seem to have any idea of how small they are in comparison. I'm going to end up being savaged by a Rottweiler in the park because the Westie will attack it, the Rottweiler will eat it and munch its way up the leash to my arm like swallowing a piece of spaghetti.

But dogs do give you unconditional love and a life-time of fun. It's just deciding which sort. I could always go to the pound and see what they've got. As long as it's smarter than my cat ...

A collie will round people up and keep them in one corner

My life as a cat

Apart from licking myself all over, it was pretty good

The Christmas holiday is stretching out before us. It's a time of year when I like to relax, once the over-eating, over-drinking and over-use of words beginning in 'over' is over. I had more time on my hands than usual a while back, and decided that to relax properly you could do a lot worse than be a cat. So I followed my cat around for a day, trying to get inside his head so that now you, too, can benefit from the experience. Here's what to expect, based on My Life as a Cat.

8.30-ish: I wake up, yawn, stretch, and attempt to pluck the carpet, but my nails are too short. I sit by the door to the laundry waiting for someone to fill my food bowl. Get funny looks from partner as I rub up against her legs. She tells me I'm even weirder than usual and asks what sort of cat food I'd like. I have cereal, but imagine what it must be like eating raw meat for breakfast — only a real cat could answer that.

8.35 to 10.30: Sleep in the sun — this must be really hot with a fur coat on.

10.31: Getting too hot in the sun, so I have to move to the shade. I lie down in exactly the same position, sleeping lightly in case next-door's dog comes into the yard and chases me — he does this whether I'm pretending to be a cat or not.

2.15: I wake up, stretch and sit staring into space, trying to look mystical and all-knowing.

2.45: I'm worn out. Have to take a nap.

5.45: I wake up feeling totally refreshed and ready for action. I chase a lizard, then run at full speed across the lawn and up the tree. I realise that I shouldn't have run up the tree because it's a lot easier to climb up and I can't see any way down. I try to look as if I'm in control.

5.55: Looks as if nobody will rescue me, so I make a clumsy and very un-catlike descent. I go through the cat-flap and rub up against my amazed partner for food.

6.05: I'm fed and ready for some real fun outside — the nearer to sunset, the more active I feel. Scratch to be let out of front door but nobody lets me out so I go out of cat-flap again. (Okay, I didn't really go out of the cat-flap but I'm mimicking my cat's behaviour to the letter, remember?)

6.06: Time to lick myself all over and pretend it makes me clean, when actually I'm just covered in spit.

7.06: I move like a tiger through the undergrowth, looking for something to kill. Each step I take, the bell on my collar rings. Everything gets out of the way as if they've heard a semi-trailer coming.

7.08: I'm bored with this. I think I'll go inside again.

7.10: I make a fuss of my partner, who tells me to get out of the way and stop being so weird, I'm making the cat jealous. The cat and I eye each other territorially. He'll keep.

7.12: I go outside again. This is great, all the smells, sights and sounds — I have a much-enhanced sense of all three now I'm a cat — who wants to be inside on a perfect summer night like this? Think I'll track down that cicada and have some fun with it.

7.13: Forget the cicada. Do they have to be that loud?

Humans may think cicadas are loud, but to a cat it's like living under an airport flight path.

7.14: Back inside, I'm ready for a serious fuss. The partner says my purring sounds vaguely disgusting and I should either blow my nose or shut up, so I go outside again. I sit at the end of the path and watch what people are doing in the street. I'm on the lookout for other cats, which I must fight if they come anywhere near my territory. None do, lucky for them. I fall asleep.

8.15: It's dark and I can see! It's cool being a cat, I'm totally unrestricted by night — unlike mere humans. There's a world of possibilities outside when you can see it all as if it's still daylight — it's scary.

8.18: Back inside, the telly is on, all seems very safe, think I'll stay here for a while.

8.21: I want to go outside again. I scratch at the lounge-room door until my partner lets me out. People don't understand our needs. You'd think they didn't understand a word we meow but that's impossible. How could they listen to us every day and not understand something? They'd have to be either really stupid or just not care.

8.23: I'm outside again. Things are rustling in the undergrowth, I can smell other cats on the prowl, time for some real action. Feeling a bit tired, though.

8.35: Back inside, scratch to be let in. It's been a big day. It's time for bed.

Not a bad life, eh? Apart from licking yourself all over, and imagine doing that with fur covering you! So, if it's relaxation you're after, spend a day as a cat this Christmas. If running around, backyard cricket and clamouring for attention are more your pace, did I ever tell you about My Life as a Dog?

The rabbit or the egg?

The meaning of Easter seems to be getting a tad lost

Most kids hear the word Easter and think eggs — real ones, raw, hard-boiled or painted but preferably chocolate, full of lollies. And the Easter Bunny. Now that's a strange one. Another example of us copying the northern hemisphere, like that red-suited Finn going 'Yo-ho-ho' in our shopping centres every Christmas.

Easter's in the northern spring, which is when rabbits have their litters. None too relevant to an Aussie autumn, but we're stuck with it, so bunnies it is. We've already got the big bunny suits, so it's a bit late to change now. And it's a chance for actors to avoid typecasting. Although I did once hear a muffled 'Yo-ho-ho' from one overheated Easter Bunny outside a World 4 Kids.

But it is a funny thing for Aussies to get behind. Rabbits have caused incredible damage to our land. Not that it's the rabbits' fault they went feral. They wanted to be kept as pets, not set free. They needed shelter, so they dug burrows. They needed food, so they ate everything that wasn't already dust. They acted like complete animals.

I had pet rabbits when I was a kid, several of them in fact. I used to sell the baby bunnies for pocket money. It never occurred to me that some people actually ate rabbit meat. I thought the ones I sold were going to other little kids to play with. I think my parents thought that if I had a breeding pair of rabbits, I wouldn't ask them awkward questions about where babies came from. I could draw my own conclusions. I did. Clearly, babies came from rabbits.

I witnessed all parts of the breeding cycle, but at eight years old I didn't put them together in the right order. I thought the crucial moment was when the doe made a huge nest at the back of the hutch from her own fur. The baby bunnies were there soon after. All that stuff with the buck and doe in the same hutch for what looked like a wrestling match was so much earlier, I didn't think it had anything to do with it. It wasn't even much of a contest as I recall; the buck always held the doe in what looked a bit like a full Nelson. I couldn't be sure. I thought the buck won because he was a boy and better at wrestling.

My favourite rabbit of all time was a New Zealand White by the name of Timmy. So what does a rabbit do to win our affections? Compared with a dog or a cat, not a hell of a lot. An ability to nibble on a piece of lettuce you're still holding in your hand seems pretty impressive. It's a rabbit — it's not likely to fetch rolled-up newspapers or chase balls of wool. And Timmy certainly bred like a rabbit. But if the guinea pig had arrived in the northern hemisphere a few centuries earlier, the phrase 'breed like rabbits' may never have been coined. We'd say 'breed like guinea pigs', because nothing breeds as fast as a guinea pig.

Someone I thought of as a friend sold me a breeding pair of guinea pigs called Bonnie and Clyde. Within a year, I had sixty-four guinea pigs. I thought I was separating males from females, but they are so difficult to sex accurately and reach sexual maturity so quickly it was often too late. It was a nightmare. You couldn't sell them — every other kid at school had as many as you did. We were all traumatised. We didn't have time for homework. We all had to dash home and find things to make new hutches from. I converted chicken crates, a chest of drawers, orange crates — my mother drew the line at me measuring up the kitchen cupboards. There was a sudden shortage of chicken wire as all the kids for miles tried to contain the guinea pig plague.

Keeping them fed was a full-time job — I tried to use it as an excuse to leave school at eleven years old to be a guinea-pig farmer. I don't remember what happened to them all. I've suppressed the memory — only therapy could bring it back. Guinea pigs are short-lived anyway and the inbreeding wouldn't have helped. I know we didn't kill any. But I do remember the sense of relief when the last one died after three years or so. I didn't even think of replacing it. I'd rather have had a breeding pair of locusts; at least one swarm and they'd have disappeared.

So that, boys and girls, is why we have the Easter Bunny and not the Easter Guinea Pig. Which is lucky really, because rabbits are bigger and have long ears, and you know what that means — more chocolate.

In search of a better bug

We need just one super-beneficial insect

I've turned over a new leaf — in fact, several new leaves. I wish I hadn't. Lacebugs, aphids, all sorts of larvae are laughing at me. Unlikely, I know, but it feels as though they are. It could be just the sound of their jaws slapping together as my plants are eaten alive.

We did a bit of remodelling of the garden in spring, so I've become more protective of my plants of late. I used to adopt a survival-of-the-fittest policy — if it can't survive our seasons without constant watering and spraying, then it doesn't belong in my garden. All that's changed, though. When you've lovingly planted a vibrant young shrub, taken it out of its pot for the last time, ruffled its roots and nestled it in compost and cow manure, you're bound to care more.

When it comes to insects, I've always believed that if you don't fiddle with the food chain they'll all eat each other and leave your plants — and you — alone. Unfortunately, nature seems out of balance in our backyard. I don't know whether it's our blue-tongue lizard, Barry, who lives behind the shed. Maybe he's eaten something which has allowed every nasty beastie below it on the food chain to flourish. Maybe it's the ants I gleefully destroyed last year. All I know is I've got lemons which look like barnacle-encrusted rocks.

I know I'll have to resort to sprays, but the thing about science is that it goes for the quick fix. You may remember the kids at school who liked to show off in chemistry class by making things explode and setting off the fire alarm. You don't think they went on to work in a bank, do you? No, they're the ones coming up with the chemicals to kill specific bugs. They didn't care about the consequences then, and they don't now. If a beneficial bug is killed in the process, it means as little to them as setting alight Smelly Kelly's tie with a Bunsen burner.

And then there are the botanists; they're just as bad. They spend their lives fiddling with the glamour part of the profession, cross-breeding and grafting to make new species of plants so they can name them after themselves. Meanwhile, the insects look forward to sampling the new addition to their menu: 'I understand it's a slightly crisper leaf, just a hint of bitterness, very good with balsamic vinegar and shredded parmesan.'

I don't want to use chemicals willy-nilly, but if a man has to buy lemons for his gin and tonic when they grow in his backyard, something's got to give. The beneficial insects aren't there, there aren't enough of them or they have so much food to choose from that they only eat the bad ones for half an hour and take the rest of the day off for a snooze in the sun.

The other thing about beneficial insects is how to tell the good guys from the bad guys — it's not as though they wear white hats. Even if they did, you'd need a microscope to see them. This is where my connection with *Better Homes and Gardens* comes in handy. I'd send the gardening editors small bugs in matchboxes for identification purposes. They asked me not to, but I'm a desperate man. I've had to stop sending them now; apparently that's the point of a restraining order. But I still stand outside on the street yelling descriptions of my lemons up at their office window: 'I think it's some kind of fungus. They've got this horrible dark-brown scabby stuff all over the skin — it doesn't go through to the fleshy part but it's driving me crazy!' I get some funny looks from people walking past, I can tell you.

If we can clone a sheep — and let's face it, we're really short of sheep, aren't we? — then surely we can fiddle with some DNA and come up with just one super-beneficial insect. It would have the speed of thought and grace of the praying mantis, the dogged persistence of the parasitic wasp and the insecticidal tendencies of the assassin bug. I think it should be a wasp, with a loud buzz so we have time to get out of the way. And if we could make it furry, like a bee, it could give the leaves a shine while it's eating the bad guys.

And while the scientists are making that one, maybe they could turn their attention to a faster compost worm. I'm tired of waiting weeks for compost. We need a better, faster, hungrier worm, one with teeth — so it can eat and digest plastic and broken light globes. Maybe it could have spikes, like an echidna, to cut through the garbage faster. I want to be able to hear munching sounds coming from my compost bin when I'm twenty metres away. So come on, guys, let's have a faster, sharper compost worm for the new millennium — the Composter 2001! Then you could have a bucket of compost worms in the office instead of a shredder.

I want to hear munching sounds from my composter

8

Handy Hints for a Relaxed and Comfortable Life

*A*ustralians long for a leader of great vision and charisma. Until then, there's John Howard. Mr Howard managed to capture the mood of the nation when he told us that he does have a vision. He wants us to be relaxed and comfortable. Like that favourite pair of winter tracky daks.

This chapter should help those of you who want to achieve John Howard's nirvana (no, it's not a cover band).

Handling your handyman

My editor at *Better Homes and Gardens* asked me to help a reader who wanted to know how to get her husband to do some projects. 'What star sign is he?' I asked, hoping the editor would find someone else. (Some blokes still haven't forgiven me for letting women in on our secret love of lawnmowing.) But she insisted, so sorry, fellas, I'm over a barrel here.

Encouragement

Flattery will get you everywhere. You will need to build his confidence — think of him as a puppy but, hopefully, house-trained. Self-assembly shelves are a good start. A two-year-old could put them together, but if you say 'They look great' and 'You're so clever' often enough, your man will be making a potting bench in no time. And even if it looks and behaves like a seesaw, the longest you have to wait for a council clean-up day is three months.

Do it yourself

It's a rare man who can see his wife with a power-drill in her hand and not want to take over. You need to achieve just the right balance of 'I can manage quite well on my own' and 'It all spins around when I start the drill'. It will only be ten minutes before he is tutting over the instructions. The occasional beer and encouraging words (see 'Encouragement'), and your project will be his project. This proves the difference between the sexes: men think working with power-tools and getting dirty is glamorous; women know we're one socket short of a set.

Shame

If you have a handyman neighbour, use him to drive your man to one of the seven deadly sins ... pride. Tell your man that you're going to ask the neighbour around to have a crack at paving the drive. This will be all the encouragement the average territorial male needs to leap into action and show that anything Jones can do, he can do better. But beware male bonding. If they start working together, they become each other's alibi: they'll both say 'Just going next door to help with the home office conversion' and slip off to the footy together.

Seduction

Tell him you have this fantasy you want to fulfil. He's making a dining table and when he's finished you make mad, passionate love on it. This should get him in the mood for a bit of woodwork and will also ensure that he makes a table that's strong enough to last a lifetime.

Shed

It's amazing the positive effect it has on some blokes to have their own shed. It's the place where they feel free to be themselves, but it also encourages creativity. The fact that they can have girlie calendars and can clear up when they want, if at all, means that they'll undertake ambitious projects at the drop of a hint and a promise to top up the beer fridge. They'll also try to eat, watch TV and sleep in there if you'll let them — it's your choice whether this is good or bad.

Bribery

Some men will try to weasel out of a project by listing the specialist equipment they'd need to, say, build a sofa. Call his bluff. Tell him you can afford it and go with him to buy the gear.

If you're not there to keep his mind on the right tools for the job, he'll be out the door with the latest car wax, sheepskin-buffing attachment for his drill and high-pressure water-jet nozzle before you can say, 'What do we need that for?' Keep a list of what he's bought. Then, when it's time to renovate the kitchen and he says he doesn't have the right tools for a job, you'll know whether he's telling the truth. Three lies is worth a pergola.

The headache

If you have to resort to this, you're married to one shameless couch potato. Issue an ultimatum: no project, no loving favours. He won't last long, particularly if it's close to a full moon. Just keep pointing to the *BH&G* page showing the project you desire. I beg you, please make this your last resort. And don't tell your old man where the idea came from ... did I mention that's not my real name on the cover of this book?

Nice guys

We all have a mate who seems to be constantly in the doghouse. He can never come out with the boys because he 'can't get a pass'. For those who want the woman in their lives to say 'Yes' when she'd usually say 'No', for those who have fallen from favour, for all those who dare to dream, here's how to turn a woman of stone into a real softie — without getting gravel rash.

Chores

If you're one of the lucky souls who doesn't already wash up, you'll be stunned at the effect it can have. She'll be putty in your hands. Women find men in rubber gloves sexier than a Fabio book cover and I don't even want to think about why. And there's vacuuming. At least a vacuum has a motor in it. And it can be fun. Sprinkle a bit of ash on the carpet, change attachments, do the bowling-ball test (as seen on TV), then empty the dust-bag in the middle of the carpet and start again. The key to scoring with chores is to be spontaneous. Don't announce it the previous day, as though it will be an event worth selling tickets to, just do it.

Do the shopping

But be careful, some supermarkets are hunting-grounds for single women. You don't want distractions like that when you're trying to remember the softest brand of toilet paper. The only way to ruin your good work is to give your regular shopper tips on how she could save money the next time she's driving the trolley.

Fix things

Women don't think like us when it comes to what's important around the home. We like to do Cape Cod conversions, extensions, granny flats — all they want is a tap that doesn't drip and a laundry drain that doesn't flood every second load of washing. So, what bothers her? The blown light-globe in the hall, the sticking bedroom window? Fix it. Don't be surprised if she cries with pleasure. You never knew foreplay was this easy, did you?

Buy flowers

Are you mad? Have you learned nothing? Buying flowers is for desperate apologies of the 'I'd had too much to drink, she meant nothing' variety. You should not use flowers for anything but emergencies or you devalue them. Give her flowers more than a couple of times a year, and she'll expect them. Then you're into heavy flower abuse: baskets of flowers, then baskets of flowers with balloons attached, until you have to give her the Goodyear blimp with a full-sized camellia tree to make an impact.

Make a date

A guaranteed winner. This can get you back in favour if you've totalled the car, run over the cat and told your boss where to stick his job. If you have kids, organise a babysitter; if you don't, use the money you save on a good bottle of wine — not screwtop or cask. Book a restaurant, one you know she likes. If you're not sure, avoid places with all-you-can-eat signs — they tend not to be too romantic. When she arrives home, give her a single red rose. At the restaurant, don't flinch when she orders the most expensive thing on the menu. Compliment her on everything you can think of — trust me, you can't overdo this — and listen. And agree when she wants you to and disagree when she wants you to — I said to listen! Pay with the credit card that isn't up to the limit and you're home free. Best thing is, you'll probably enjoy it yourself.

Give her a lie-in

If you only do this on Mother's Day, expect to come home one day to find your wife has moved, or has

How to become the sexiest man ever to walk the earth

changed the locks and taken out a restraining order. Switch off the alarm, sneak out of bed — saving all your early-morning noises until you close the bedroom door — get the kids ready for school and make her breakfast. It's easy. The real advantage of the lie-in is that she loves you for the whole day. By the time you see her that night, you'll have grown in her imagination into the kindest, sexiest man ever to walk the earth. Not bad for toasting a bit of multigrain and pouring hot water on some coffee granules!

Let's get physical

It's nearly summer — and the moment of truth

Pants a bit tight, fellas? Those shirts shrunk in the wash? Yes, you've piled it on over winter and it's time to get the polo shirts and shorts out of the bottom drawer. Two more unforgiving garments have never been made. Every Super Supreme pizza and double cheesy-weezy-burger-bacon-chicken-zingy-wingy combo meal can be seen straining at the fabric ... it's time to shape up for summer.

You could go to the gym, but when you've got a house and garden it can seem like a gross dereliction of duty to pedal on an exercise bike when the grass is high enough to tickle a horse's fancy. So here's your cut-out-and-keep work-out! Sorry there's no accompanying video, but the powers-that-be thought the sight of my backside in a pair of shorts was unlikely to sell many copies.

Warm-ups

These are essential so you don't pull muscles or split your clothing and shock the kiddies across the road.

Wheelbarrow squats. Hold the handles of your wheelbarrow, keep your back straight and bend your knees until your thighs are horizontal. (If you live on a sloping block and can't keep an eye on the horizon, use a spirit level.) Now stand up, keeping your arms straight down by your side. Depending on your height, when you're about halfway up you'll be lifting the barrow. Ten repeats. Works the hamstrings a treat — probably why builders can't keep their bums completely in their shorts. As you get fitter, add the weight of one small child in the barrow each month.

You'll soon have hamstrings like a kangaroo

Shoulder stretches. Dip your yard brush in a solution of dishwashing liquid and water and stand under the eaves of your house. Now raise the brush over your head and brush the dirt off the soffit boards. Do about half a metre right-handed, then swap for the next half metre. Build up gradually. After two weeks, use a paintbrush instead and paint your soffit boards. At this stage, you may like to wear a hat or you could look as if you've lost a fight with a seagull.

Main exercise

The Victa upper body exercise. You will need one lawn-mower (petrol, rotary, vroom vroom!) with grass-catcher and a compost heap or bin (optional). Cut your grass until your catcher is full. Stop the mower at the furthest possible point from where you intend putting the cuttings. Now detach the catcher with your right hand and carry it to the compost bin. Empty the catcher by supporting the top of it with the left hand and tipping it with the right. Repeat the process left-handed for the next full catcher. Continue until the lawn is completed. Ignore the laughter of loved ones — I'm sure Arnie Schwarzenegger's folks once laughed at him.

The quadra-quad tune-up. You will need the lawn-mower, a tank of petrol, a full grass-catcher and some bricks. Put a brick on the flat bit of mower behind the engine and push. If it's too easy add another brick. Feel those muscles working in the wallet–pocket area — you'll soon have hamstrings like a kangaroo. You've overdone the number of bricks if you start rotivating the lawn instead of mowing it.

Stepladder aerobics. A good indoor one for rainy days. Climb the ladder a step at a time, returning to the ground between each extra step climbed. By the time you're standing on the top step, you should be breathing heavily. Always carry a light-globe with you in case you find any that need changing. And for advanced exercise (only for fit blokes or preferably their wives or girlfriends): paint the ceiling.

The sweep. The reason so many of us are out of shape is that instead of being sensible and sweeping our paths, we stand around playing our hoses on them. Some pretend there's a purpose to this madness by using a high-pressure hose attachment; and as for weed-blowers, don't get me started!

Be a man — sweep with a yard broom. Change hands halfway through. It's the quickest method known to man and is great for the chest and upper arms.

The cool-down

Essential so you don't wind up stiff as a board the next day.

The dog run. Put the family dog on a long rope. Tie one end to the Hills Hoist; the dog should be free to run in a circle without hitting his head on too many hard objects. Now, whatever he hates most, try to do. If it's bathing, chase him with the soap and bucket. If it's brushing, the brush — you get the idea. If you end up with a clean, brushed dog, you've one exercise left.

The fridge door swing. Slowly open the fridge door and, keeping the back straight, bend with your knees and take out a bottle of beer in your right hand. Stand up. Twist off the top using your left hand, tilt your head back and pour beer into your mouth. See, you feel in great shape already!

How to get the breaks this Christmas

Christmas is not about martyrdom ... that's Easter. You've worked all year to earn a good time, so make sure you have it. Follow these tips to get the best out of your festive season.

While you're at home

Decorations. Bung some lights on anything resembling a tree in the front yard. Switch them on at night. That's it, you've decorated. Do not put fake ice on windows or cottonwool snow on anything. It's silly. If it has ever snowed in lowland Australia on 25 December, I like knitting.

Rewrite the Santa Clause. Americans may have perfected Santa Claus with his white beard, red wool suit and fur trim, but shouldn't we Australians have come up with a summer version? I suggest Swag Man.

Tell the kids that Santa is busy in the north and if he comes down under he'll overheat and die, so Swag Man's taking over the franchise. He wears a brown Akubra, blue singlet and long baggy shorts. He spends all winter under Uluru with his merry dingoes and then at Christmas gets in his huge white four-wheel-drive Holden and sets off through the red dust to deliver presents. If the kids leave a light beer and a piece of cold pizza under the barbecue, he'll give them a gift. But only if they've been good ... and that means a minimum of five consecutive days and a promise to tidy their rooms till they leave home or can afford their own cleaner.

The Christmas dinner. We all know this means slaving over a hot stove ... Wake up, Australia, it's the middle of summer. Just because your grandparents wanted to have a northern hemisphere Christmas doesn't mean you do. Forget turkey, unless it's cold. I'm talking seafood, cold meats, pasta and rice salads, pavlova, fruit salad, ice cream, sorbet. Buy them all at the supermarket, or make them a few days before and freeze them. Christmas dinner? No sweat. And drink in moderation — difficult to define, but generally speaking, if you wake up and you've got a glass in your hand you're overdoing it.

Pressies. Get the kids toys, get each other sexy underwear, give charity donations on behalf of everyone else and tell them in their Christmas card.

Pool-sit. Only offer to keep an 'eye on the house' for neighbours who have a pool. You can keep an eye as you float with a cocktail in your hand. First make sure the pool filters work or the whole thing can turn to green slime overnight and no amount of chlorine will fix it. I know, it happened to me.

Avoid family arguments. Tell your in-laws you're going away for Christmas and leave the answering machine on to screen calls. You can all laugh at Aunty Eileen as she tries to leave a message.

When you're away

Going away. Time your holiday so you're at home watching the cricket when every other parent is on the road with the kids asking them how far it is to the next McDonalds. Important words to look for in holiday brochures when booking are 'child-minding facilities', 'TV and video' (in case it rains), 'all meals included' and 'mini bar'. And if you do drive a long distance, stop, revive, survive ... and take some toilet paper.

Be honest. You pay good money in taxes for your children's education. When they ask 'What's that fish?' or 'How far now?' tell them the truth: 'You've got as much idea as I have.' Let their teachers tell them next term. With any luck, your offspring will realise that you're as much use as a beached whale and they'll take control of their own entertainment. As long as this doesn't involve swimming out of their depth, native wildlife or spear-guns, what harm can it do?

Avoid burglary. Record your neighbour's dog as it barks for the ten hours a day that its owners are at work. Get a time switch. Time the hi-fi to play the tape of the dog barking every night from 10 p.m. to 8 a.m. Telephone from your resort and order pizza and taxis to go to your home ... burglars will either think you're at home or that it's a meal stop for taxi drivers.

Beer in the twin-tub

Don't throw out old household appliances, recycle them instead

Fondue sets. Twin-tubs. Paul Keating. They have something in common. They were all something we thought we needed and now we don't. I've been feeling a bit green of late and it's not just due to mould. We're becoming a throw-away society, whereas some old household items could — with a bit of imagination, plenty of gaffer tape and a total disregard for safety — be put to good use.

Before you try any of these suggestions yourself, please note that the publisher and I accept no responsibility for severed limbs, melted power circuits or lost pets. Here are my thoughts, in no particular order of importance. If you have any better (i.e. funny) suggestions, send them in. God knows I could use a laugh — I turn forty next month.

The fondue set

If it still works, it can come in handy when you've got a cold. Fill with water, some vapour rub, simmer, then breathe in the steam with a towel draped over your head.

Jaffle-maker

Such beautiful craftsmanship shouldn't be thrown away just because the electrics are so shot that the street lights dim when you switch it on. Use it as a really shallow jelly mould. The resulting jelly is ideal for putting in the kids' peanut-butter sangers. Isn't that what the Yanks do? Alternatively, use it to make your own giant ravioli. Four ravioli pillows serve four hungry people.

Twin-tubs

These are ideal ice-buckets for big entertainers. Simply put beer in the washing tub, wine in the dryer.

Tumble-dryer

The perfect piece of exercise equipment for an over-active hamster. Or an electrically operated lettuce-dryer for really big salads.

Fridge

Always wanted a dishwasher, but never had the space? Move the fridge to a well-drained area in the backyard. Punch a hole in the back big enough to take the diameter of a garden hose, put the hose through the hole and attach the spinkler attachment. Now stack your dirty plates inside, sprinkle some dishwashing powder in the butter compartment, close the door and turn on the hose. You may need to use some packing tape to secure the door properly. And it's not suitable for glassware, crockery or anything breakable. But your Tupperware will thank you.

Video recorder

Your two-year-old was right. Once it's packed up, the VCR is only good for shoving stale bits of toast into.

Hills Hoist

Don't throw away the old one just because it's a dirty old aluminum one and won't fold up. Make a bit of a tower for it nearby, then cut off the main post near the ground. Now take the whole hoist, turn it on its side and mount it on top of the tower. You've got yourself the makings of a windmill. Add a few old pairs of tracky daks to catch the wind, some cogs, a magneto and you'll be selling electricity to the national grid. Or mount it on a board, have the kids write some prizes on bits of old card, peg them to the line and they can play Wheel of Fortune (top-dollar saving there!).

Television

If you're lucky enough to have one of the old timber-veneer TVs, dump the workings in the bin and you've got a rabbit hutch, ant farm or any pet container you fancy. You'll need chicken wire and/or glass if you actually want Floppy Ears to stay put. If it's a portable telly, better still. This means you can take the cat to the vet in it.

Lawnmower

If you really can't get any more happy hours of mowing out of it, bury it under its favourite tree.

Washboard

If Gran's still got one of these hanging around, you can be a fifth of a Zydeco band (you know, that foot-stompin' swamp music from New Orleans). Grab yourself a few thimbles, sit the washboard on your lap, make like you're scratching your belly, and bingo, you're listening to the sound of music.

So, next council clean-up day I don't want to see anything but an old mattress on your nature strip. (Once their springs have sprung, the only good place for them is the dump. On second thoughts, better hang on to it for now and I'll get back to you.) And start saving string: you're going to need a lot of it.

The lie-in, the switch and the wardrobe

We spend a third of our lives in bed, on average. If you average out the seven hours a night that men sleep with the nine hours women seem to need, you get eight. There are 24 hours in a day, 1000 metres in a kilometre and three coins in a fountain — look, take my word for it, it's a third, or 0.333 recurring for the pedantic.

If you feel you're being short-changed, skip breakfast. If you feel you're wasting your life sleeping, join the club. I don't think we spend enough time thinking about our bedrooms. They're a lot more than just a room to sleep in. It's a room where you can let go of your inhibitions and be really, really wicked. Yes, it's a room to eat in. It's one of life's most indulgent pleasures to take your breakfast back to bed and luxuriate in the decadence of it all, particularly at this time of the year when the early mornings can be a tad brisk. In fact, this house is so cold breakfast in bed is a necessity, not a luxury.

You can watch television from bed too. It's great, but you must make sure you've positioned the telly high enough or you have to flatten your feet to see the screen and then you get a cramp just as you get to the good bit. But generally beds are great for television watching, because you've got all that quilt space to stack however many remote controls you need to operate the telly, video and cable TV. Yes, I recommend cable TV for the bedroom, because if you can't be bothered to get out of bed you probably don't care that much about quality either. You can channel-surf when you get bored, and even if you do, what's the worst that can happen, you fall asleep?

I have a fantasy bedroom. No, girls, it isn't full of pillows and flowers and candles and cuddly toys. It's more like the ultimate five-star hotel experience. First, I want to have all the switches that control everything in the room right next to my pillow. That's what you get in flash hotels. Main light? The switch is right there. Air-conditioning? Move your finger slightly and on it comes. Ice-cold beer? Get real, this is a fantasy bedroom, not Fantasy Island.

Then there's the ensuite bathroom. Some of you may have these, but I don't and I want one so badly I'm thinking of taking up the whole second bedroom just to make it happen. Guys love the ensuite; the shorter that first walk of the day or in the middle of the night, the better. And, of course, it should have spa jets in the bath and a phone you can use in the bath, on the toilet and even in the shower so you can share your singing with anyone on speed dial. But my fantasy bathroom won't have those bright lights over the mirror that make even a bushy-haired man like me look as if he's thinning on top.

Back in the bedroom there are a few more pieces of sophistication that I'd like. A mini-bar, just like in hotels, with little spirits bottles, bags of cashews, a brand of chips you've never heard of and a small Toblerone. You could even have a pretend price list and laugh 'All on the company!' as you help yourself to a $6 bottle of beer. Of course, there should be a selection of new-release videos to choose from. If you're relying on cable television, you probably need both Optus and Foxtel just to be sure. And ideally you should have a live-in, dependent relative who provides room service when you fancy a club sandwich at two in the morning.

It doesn't stop there. My fantasy bedroom would go further than some fancy five-star hotel room. You know those lights on the floor of aircraft that the flight attendants point to when they tell you how you're going to get out of the darkened cabin in the unlikely event of total disaster? Well, I want those lights all down my side of the bed, so the next time I check that the possums only sound as though they've fallen through the roof, I won't stub my toe on a bed leg on my return.

The bed itself should have an electric blanket for winter but, get this ... an electric cooling blanket for summer. I know, it's brilliant — I amaze myself sometimes! Finally, the bed should be adjustable so that if you want to sit up, you press the handset and the whole mattress lifts, as you see in American hospital dramas. I could be happy spending a third of my life in a room like that. With a bedside table for my computer I could spend half my life there. If my writing seems more laid-back from here on in, you know why.

The twelve rules of Christmas

How to avoid the pitfalls of the season

It may take a lifetime of experience to nail down a really great Christmas. This is a shortcut to help you have one this year. (There's no particular religious significance to the fact that there are twelve rules.)

1   Never buy a real tree

It's worth warning those poor souls who think that a real Christmas tree is best. Pine needles are impossible to get rid of: they leave a trail when you take out the tree to throw it away, they are sharp, they like to stick in the soles of your feet and make you jump a metre in the air when you're carrying a cup of coffee or glass of red wine. You have been warned.

2   Beware the champagne breakfast

It can seem like a good idea to blow away the Christmas Eve cobwebs with some bubbly. But you won't think it's so smart when guests start to arrive, you're still in your boxers and T-shirt, the lounge is full of torn wrapping paper and the turkey's been in the oven for three hours but you forgot to light the gas.

3   Never try a new recipe

This is not the day of the year to try to impress with Turkey à la Pesto or Tandoori Ham. People like their

Christmas lunch to be the same every year. They know they've got to eat masses of food and the last thing they want to do is worry about whether or not they like it. I know, my Honey Butterfly Prawns went down like a lead balloon — and those butterflies took ages to catch.

4   Be flexible

It's inevitable that if you plan an outdoor Christmas it will rain and if you plan to eat inside the temperature will be 40°C in the shade. You should be prepared to eat hot or cold food, in or out, any time from midday to midnight.

5   Don't drive

Christmas Day is World's Worst Drivers' Day on the roads, because a lot of them haven't driven since last Christmas. People who couldn't be trusted even to sit safely in the front passenger seat on any other day of the year are suddenly designated drivers.

6   Don't give alcohol as a gift

There's always one rellie who can't be trusted to limit himself to the same number of drinks as everyone else. If you make the mistake of giving him a bottle of Scotch for a present, he'll have the cap off and be knocking it back before you can say: 'Has anyone seen where Uncle Billy's gone?' He'll be in the shed, singing songs rated M for mature audiences featuring high level coarse language and frequent sexual references.

7   Avoid remote-controlled toys

Kids love remote-controlled cars — until the batteries run out on Boxing Day. But they're not the best to have whizzing around your feet when you're carrying scalding-hot dishes of vegetables and gravy. Avoid broken legs, burnt heads and ruined furniture by giving toys that aren't self-propelling. These, however, can still be tripped over, so keep directions to the nearest hospital on the fridge door.

8 Guard the phone

People love a catch-up with far-flung relatives on Christmas Day, but tend to forget that by the time everyone at your end has had a word with everyone at the other end, the cost is heaps more than the 'Don't worry about it' that you confidently said with post-lunch bonhomie. And don't forget your kids like to win the great 'I've got better and more expensive presents than you' race and will phone Jake on holiday in Greece to make sure.

9 Keep a well-stocked medicine cabinet

There will be cuts, burns, indigestion and hangovers, so be prepared. Vitamin C is for Christmas.

10 Beware the glass half-empty

No, I don't mean keep everyone topped up, I mean don't leave half-empty glasses unattended. Kids just want to be like you, so they're bound to sneak a try. And you really don't want to have to explain to the irritable doctor who's been stuck with the Christmas Day shift at Casualty why your nine-year-old appears to be drunker than Uncle Billy.

11 Don't forget your pets

Your pets know it's Christmas and expect you to make a bit of an effort for them, too. Fresh meat is a favourite, a bone for Prince, maybe a bit of topside mince for Felix. If you ignore them, they will have their revenge. Many a turkey has been dragged from the table by a dog that's been taken for granted. And the best-behaved cat can be relied upon to jump into the middle of the table and walk across everyone's plate.

12 Have a box of tissues ready

The girls do tend to get emotional at this special time. One of them will mention how she misses her dear-departed husband, parent or dog, and the tears will flow. This is the cue for the men to squeeze in one more over of backyard cricket and talk about engines, lawnmowers and who's going to win the Boxing Day Cricket Test.

Beware self-propelled cars

Home from home

For a lot of men, SOHO is secret bloke's code for 'indoor shed'

As you know, SOHO is jargon for small office/home office. I am in one as I write and, like many men, I love it. 'Just off to catch up with some paperwork,' we say. Then it's on with the computer and onto the Internet, and a slow search for the *Baywatch* homepage. Or a quick play on the flight simulator. Sometimes I surf the Net in between writing a column (lucky I write for a monthly magazine).

It wasn't so long ago that a home office was a writing desk in the corner of the lounge-room, preferably a bureau so you could put up the lid and hide the unfinished letters, bills and Tim Tams. Nowadays it's a whole room dedicated to technology. My own humble SOHO has two PCs, a printer, modem, answering machine, fax machine, filing cabinet, shelves, a fan for summer, a heater for winter and a mini hi-fi. And a pencil sharpener to remind me how simple life was before electricity, Telstra and Microsoft.

Working from home isn't for everybody. I'm pleased about this. I don't want to have to go to someone else's house for petrol or a loaf of bread. But if you do work at home, feng-shui expert Howard Choy reckons it's a good idea actually to take a walk around the block in the morning before settling down in your office. This helps your brain separate home from the workplace, so you sit down and get straight into work instead of giving the dog a flea bath. It makes a lot of sense but, sadly, it would mean dressing and shaving. Think I'll stick with walking straight from the bathroom to the office with wet hair, a towel round my waist and flossing my teeth. My neighbours don't need to see me walking around like that when they've just had breakfast.

There were two major findings from my extensive research into SOHOs. One is that a whole lot of time wasting goes on. The other is that, like grass, the SOHO's always better on the other side of the fence. I'm actually pretty disciplined in my office and mostly I work … but this is not always so. There are many games that grown men can play on computers. Most are like the games that young boys play, only not as violent. There are even games that allow you to be the coach of a football team; every man thinks he could do a better job than the real coach, and with the computer's help, you can prove it. Although when your team hits a losing streak and the board sacks you it's as devastating as in real life. Look, it wasn't my fault, there were injuries to key players and I didn't have the money to buy any more because I decided to build a new stadium. Those pretend newspaper headlines can be so cruel.

And then there's the biggest time waster since the Rubik's cube — the Internet. It contains every bit of trivia you could ever want — ninety per cent of which is spelt incorrectly and who-knows-what per cent of which is wrong. But that doesn't stop us from surfing it, any more than huge seas and gales stop real surfers.

My office could, if you were very kind, be called cheap and cheerful. Or, as some guests of our boundless hospitality said, 'What do they say? Messy desk, creative mind?' or 'Have you been burgled?'

So I am always amazed at what others can achieve with a similar floor area and a brutal attitude to unwanted paper. My perfect friends — they of the renovated house, angelic daughter and subfloor sub-woofer — have an office so beautifully appointed you don't realise it is one until you see the computer screen in the corner and a discreetly placed fax machine. It's a bit like when you go into people's homes and think they haven't got a telly until they open a cupboard to reveal their guilty secret: a 68-centimetre-wide screen with surround sound and Dolby.

My office could look like that — with a bit of work. I'll get right onto it in a minute or two. But now I've finished this bit, I just have to coach the Socceroos against Italy in the World Cup Final. Then I'll have a walk around the block and come home from the office — it's been a hard day.

Bath to the future

This time, I'm ahead of the experts

You've probably read a lot about bathrooms in glossy magazines (and in this book). You may think the experts have covered all there is to know about the room in our homes which contains, by definition, the bath. Of course they have — for now. But I've designed the bathroom of the future.

The basics of a bathroom are all there already. Most of us take for granted the hot and cold running water — and flushing toilets. And electric heaters and ceiling fans. And mould in the shower cubicle. Most of us shower for a quick clean. We take baths to relax, lying flat out in a combination of hot water, bubbles and essential oils. But I'm a bloke, and even though I like all of the above, as soon as I close the bathroom door behind me I'm overcome by that most basic of male instincts. The need to read the paper. The bath-friendly newspaper with waterproof paper and ink hasn't been made yet and, let's face facts, isn't likely to be.

What we need is a bath-reader. I haven't really refined the idea, but it will be something like those page-turning machines you see in posh hospitals. It will be retractable, like indoor clothes lines. Before submerging, you'll be able to put the paper into the stand, get in the bath, then swing the bath-reader over the water. The height will be adjustable so that you can read without worrying about steamed-up glasses. The pages will be turned by a toe-operated turning device so they don't get wet. I don't think an electric page-turning system would be wise, given the distinct possibility of death by electrocution while doing the crossword.

Also, the shape of the bath needs to be changed to be more accommodating to lying down — more shoulder room, arm-rests, foot-rests and space for inflatable waterproof pillows. And a safe harbour for toy battleships and squeaky ducks. In the future, all baths will be spa baths and this will allow for the introduction, via the jet nozzles, of a constant water temperature device. This will automatically put more hot water in as the bath starts to cool, as well as keeping the water level the same. There's nothing worse than topping up with hot and having to guess how much water to let out, then lying back to discover you're no longer fully submerged. You'll be able to bath motionless for as long as you want and emerge relaxed, happy, well-read and wrinkled like a prune.

The shower cubicle of the future needs some serious thought and I've already had it. Car wash! I'm sure I'm not the only one who's sat in the car wash (in my car) and thought how great it would be to scale it all down to fit in a shower cubicle. Imagine. Step into the cubicle and stand with your toes against a foot-rest. We don't come with hand brakes, so maybe you hold onto a rail. Press a button and the red light goes green, then soapy hot water is sprayed onto your body from dozens of little nozzles. Then from the same nozzles, clean water rinses you off. Now here's the brilliant bit — hot air to dry you. I don't know why it hasn't been done already. Hotels would love it — they wouldn't need towels, so nobody could steal them.

You could even have the human equivalent of the luxury car wash, only instead of spraying you with hot wax it sprays you with body lotion. Or sunblock for the kids. I'm not sure if anyone would want the nylon brushes flailing all their skin away but, if we do go that far, remember that you'll have to ensure anything on your body resembling an aerial is fully retracted before you start. And here's another idea: the washbasin should have a rim, like on the toilet, so when you've finished shaving and have a sinkful of whiskers they just flush right away.

And all toilets will have a phone next to them, as they do in ritzy hotels. This is the pinnacle of man's achievement. Sitting on the toilet, catching up with his reading and making a phone call. Women, for some reason, can't see the attraction. All they want in the bathroom of the future is a man who changes the toilet roll when it's empty. That's not the future, that's science-fiction.

That's entertainment

You've been to parties ... now it's time to throw one

So you're thinking about doing some entertaining? Which means decisions, decisions and yet more decisions. It's no time to be indecisive ... I'm almost certain.

We like to entertain at home. I don't mean tap-dancing, although it's handy when you have forgotten to marinate the baby octopus. I mean full-on, people-round-for-the-evening kind. We cook, they eat, they drink, we cook, they leave, we wonder if they had a good time or were drunk and whether it's the same thing anyway.

Entertaining at home is evolving at an incredible rate. The days of just lighting a barbie and inviting acquaint-ances to cook their own meat on it are long gone. As are snags rolled up in white bread with tomato sauce. No, now we have to decide if we want a dinner party (bit posh), cocktail party (sounds posh but is a lot easier) or a barbie (doesn't sound posh, isn't that easy really and depends as much on weather as food to be a success).

Then there are the variations like the pool party — which is any of the above, only in and around the pool. This is much easier to pull off if you have plastic plates, cutlery and glasses, you have no shame about your body and you own a pool. There's also the kids' party where the parents, after a few beers, find themselves bouncing around in the giant inflatable castle or wrestling in sumo suits as the kids shake their heads in disgust, go inside and load the PlayStation.

There are just so many aspects to consider when you're throwing a party. Like the floor covering. Hadn't thought of that, had you? Well, if you've ever just pol-ished the floorboards and then seen the damage that several pairs of high heels can do in an evening, it's a sight you'd never forget. I knew I should have worn my favourite pair of thongs, but one thing led to another ... And carpet ... red wine — need I say more?

Then you have to decide if you want the festivities

outside, inside or a combination of both. Better to make it one or the other, or everyone you want to talk to will be outside but all the people you don't know will be with you in the kitchen when you're trying to fry the jumbo economy pack of spring rolls in one frypan. If it's outside, you have to think of all the creatures of the night, other than your mate Baz, that can give people a nasty bite. We've got a couple of those bamboo citronella lanterns. They look very Pacific Islands and stop the mozzies biting anyone over 2.5 metres tall. Any mozzie lower than that is below the fumes and continues to suck at pieces of bare flesh.

The party food isn't too important unless someone has allergies and even then, if it's a smorgasbord affair, they can work around it. But if the event is a dinner party, some subtle inquiry at the initial invitation stage can prevent that embarrassing conversation while you wait for the ambulance to arrive after an allergy-sufferer collapses purple-faced on sampling your Secret Prawn Surprise.

Friend-matching is even more important. The more the merrier isn't a cliché for nothing. The more friends you invite, the more chance you have that they'll actually like some of your other friends. Just because you like them doesn't mean everyone else will. I once had close friends nearly come to blows when they met for the first time. Not what you want at a party ... save that for Christmas day with the rellies.

Setting the mood music is another consideration. No two people like exactly the same music. Except maybe twins. And even then, sometimes one twin prefers the left speaker to the right and vice versa. The trick is volume: if the music is low enough nobody is really bothered, but you've avoided those awkward silences. If there's a lull in conversation, people can try to work out if they're listening to jazz, classical or Cold Chisel.

Once the party is in full swing, there is the constant problem of clean glasses. People drink from a glass, put it down, go to the loo, forget which one was theirs and help themselves to another one. Before you know it, twenty people have forty glasses on the go and you're serving champagne in coffee mugs.

The worst part is cleaning up the next day after they've all gone. Someone should invent a glass detector to track down the glasses and bottles tucked away in forgotten places. A cigarette-butt detector would do it, as most of the bottles and cans have doubled as ashtrays. But there's an easier way to reduce the clean-up. Don't ask people to bring a bottle, make them take one away instead.

Take the fear out of New Year

A whole New Year stretching out in front of you? I can sum it up in one word: potential. This could be the year to achieve all your goals on the home front. But don't make resolutions; you'll only break them. What you need is a plan.

You should plan to start small and work up. After all, you've got all year. So, seeing that it's hot and you don't want to get too tired so soon after Christmas, make a list. Three columns should be enough: 'Can Do In A Day', 'Can Do In A Weekend', 'Can Do In My Dreams'.

'Can Do In A Day' jobs are easy things: for instance,

making a list. You can do that in a day, have a drink and congratulate yourself on a great start to the New Year. Now, a list is a very personal thing. You don't have to show it to anybody else, but you'll know you're working to a plan, which will give you a real sense of purpose. So when you're on the sun-lounge, pen and paper at the ready and your partner asks, 'What about all this work you said you were going to do?' You can respond with a mysterious, 'I'm doing it now.'

'Can Do In A Day' jobs are mostly routine mainten-ance: lawn cutting, shrub pruning, weed pulling, gutter cleaning, window easing, door shaving — and any other problem areas you can think of. The trick with this list is to make sure the job takes a day at the absolute outside. Allow time for a stretch, plenty of refreshment breaks and checking on the sport on the telly. I know what tops off my list in this category ... my tools. I've been kidding myself that it's acceptable to keep them stuffed in boxes in the shed, but I've seen the future at a friend's house. A tool for every job, and every tool in its place, neatly hanging on a pegboard ... and he knows it's in its place because he draws around the shape of the tool in marker pen. It's a great idea, so I'll steal it. Mind you, with my lack of drawing skill I bet I still manage to put screw-drivers where I should be putting spanners.

'Can Do In A Weekend' are the larger projects. The shed-building, room-painting, patio-paving, drive-laying sorts of jobs. Those who are gluttons for renovations will willingly take on such a project every weekend, with a couple of 'Can Do In A Day' jobs on week nights as well. However, if your home is in reasonable condition — after the kids have gone to bed and the washing up is done — you don't need to bust a gutter. One weekend project a year may be enough. One a month and you could, say, paint every room in your house this year ... by spring. That would still leave three free weekends a month to visit friends and be overly sympathetic about lack of progress with their place.

So what about the 'Can Do In My Dreams' list? Whatever you put in here should be totally unobtainable. Building a large-scale model of the Opera House or the MCG, cooking the world's largest lamington, sewing a three-hectare cross-stitch of the cast of *Melrose Place*, creating the weed-free lawn — things that really would take time and skill far greater than mere mortals could hope for.

But why, oh Guru, I hear you ask, why must our dreams be so grand? Because you can do everything else in a day or a weekend. It's a only a matter of stringing a few 'Can Do In A Day' jobs together with 'Can Do In A Weekend' projects. For example, a brick garage. Forming up for a concrete floor, even on a sloping site, you can do in a weekend. Concreting the floor you can do the next weekend. Building the walls a bricklayer will string out — literally — for a week. If you've got the skills, it would take a weekend, two if it's big and you get rained off. The roof, if you use timber with aluminium sheeting, a weekend or so. Fixing up doors, a day at the most. You don't even have to do it on consecutive weekends. It's what builders call programming, it's what the rest of us call not biting off more than you can chew. Remember, Rome wasn't built in a day ... and the Romans didn't have test matches and New Year sales to distract them.

So, your list for the year can be a wish list. Do the 'Can Do In A Day' stuff for a few weeks and you'll find no task is too scary. And as you stand in your new attic room this time next year, you can gaze out of the window at a weed-free lawn.

Who am I kidding? You'll have to ask Santa/Swag Man for that one.

Can do in a day

Can do in my dreams

Everything and the kitchen sink

As long as you can wire a plug and change a light-globe, you should have no trouble renovating your kitchen. You can do it all yourself. *BH&G* building editor Mike Jackson* did, and a fine job he made of it.

Naturally, being an expert, he carried out a few refinements above and beyond the norm. His first problem was a slope across the floor that must have been thirty centimetres. Unwary visitors could step down into the kitchen and find themselves skidding out the back door. So he jacked up the rear of the house, by himself, of course.

He built the cupboards, fitted drawers and hung the doors, employing tradesmen only for jobs where it is a legal requirement to be licensed. And he built speakers into the walls so that at breakfast Neil Young could remind him that rock 'n' roll will never die. But for me, the best part is that he had a modern, very expensive-looking kitchen built around an original Early Kooka gas stove which blends in completely. This is why his articles were in the front of the magazine and I'm way up the back.

When I replaced my kitchen I chose the easy way, selecting the best value of three quotes from kitchen companies. They do most of the tough stuff, like measuring up, designing and installing the finished units. They'll handle everything else, for a price, but any

---

* He's no longer the building editor. He now lives in Tasmania, where he writes a fishing column for the local paper, notable for the fact that it rarely mentions fishing or even fish.

self-respecting bloke wants to get in there and have some justification for saying, 'I did that.'

I know what selling point would have made choosing the kitchen cupboards easier for me. 'Guaranteed to be cockroach-free forever.' There must be a way of designing cupboards to baffle the cockroach hordes, without soaking them in chemicals. How about miniature electric fences behind the skirtings; mazes that confuse the little devils until they give up and move next door; tiny sprung flaps that flick them onto their backs before they can get out onto worktops or in cupboards? All a dream, I fear. I suspect a conspiracy between the kitchen and surface-spray companies.

I was dreading the moment I would have to remove the old kitchen cupboards. I imagined an angry cockroach family of Mum, Dad and 10,000 kids would rush out and attack me, crawling into my shorts and scuttling over me until I went mad. I didn't see one, as it turned out. Doubtless they were tipped off by the kitchen installers.

The biggest danger I faced was taking the old units and throwing them into the skip. Not because of nails sticking out of pieces of timber, but because next-door's dog didn't appreciate my handi-skip on her favourite patch of nature strip. Every piece of laminate I threw in provoked a louder growl. She didn't bite me, though. She saved that for the kitchen installers the next day. They were not happy. 'It's not my dog,' I protested. They didn't believe me. They threw in an extra pair of breeding cockroaches behind the fridge.

Once the units were in, I cut out the worktops for the sink and cooktop using my trusty jigsaw, the finest tool in the history of electricity, no, the world. In fact, the

'On the financial front ... Kitchen sinks record a new high on the bullion exchange.'

universe. Unsurprisingly, this was after I'd bought the sink and cooktop. I foolishly spent all my lead-in time getting better and better prices for the gas oven and cooktop. The sink, I thought, couldn't cost much. I know, I'm a naive fool, but I reckoned it was just a big hole with a couple of smaller holes punched out of it. I swaggered into the appliance centre fully expecting to buy the top-of-the-range double-drainer, double-bowl, waste-disposal-included, Rolls Royce of sinks. I came out with the single-drainer, single-bowl, Leyland P76 of sinks. It was that or try to live without one until the next pay cheque.

I don't know why TV newsreaders tell us the price of gold every night. They should tell us the price of stainless steel — it's obviously a hell of a lot more valuable. And the mixer tap! Nothing so simple should cost so much. And that includes the average IOC delegate's trip to the snow.

The most satisfying parts of the renovation were the finishing touches. The wall tiling in particular — I got so into it I seriously thought about doing the ceiling too. It is so soothing, sticking on one tile at a time, pressing it until it's just right, putting the matchsticks — that's the way I do it, I like the element of danger — between it and the next one.

Kitchen renovations really aren't that stressful. One tip: if you use the matchstick method, remember to take them out before trying out the gas cooktop. It was the best indoor fireworks display I've ever seen.

'Just a short-term lease, thanks — my other cupboard's being refurbished.'

9

The Sentimental Bloke

L ike most men of my generation, I try not to dwell on the past. It's not like we had it tough. Okay, so the telly was black and white, but at least we didn't have to gather around the radio for entertainment. The rate of change is so great at the moment that it's difficult not to mourn the passing of certain icons — the vinyl album, the betamax VCR, cricket uniforms that weren't mobile advertising hoardings.

The next couple of pieces are about as sentimental as I get. Fear not, they won't leave you blubbing like Bob Hawke.

Disappearing world

Fond memories of once-newfangled inventions

It's happened. It may be one of those urban myths, but a friend assures me his seven-year-old son saw one of his dad's vinyl LP records and asked, 'What's that?' A child of the CD and cassette tape age, he saw a vinyl album, still being released here until the early nineties (and still produced as new overseas, but that's another axe to grind) and saw something as foreign as the old paper-roll phonograph would have looked to us. Soon, the indispensable items of our youth will be museum pieces — it's already happening, I tell you. If you have children, act now and educate them about some of the great things we had as kids.

Reel-to-reel tape recorders

Wonderfully cumbersome and awkward to use, but favourite uncles always had them and would record your shy five-year-old nursery-rhyme recitals on them. These were then played back to you in your early teens and were so embarrassing you wanted the ground to open and swallow you up.

8-millimetre movie cameras

The modern video camera could never have happened if it hadn't been for these. I can't remember exactly, but I think they could only record about twelve minutes on one reel. Showing films at family gatherings took forever, as a new reel was threaded onto the projector every ten or so minutes until finally sticking halfway through and melting the film. The arrival of the rellies, recently back from holidays and hauling a projector and screen, was greeted with a moan about the impending boredom.

Of course, there was no sound, which was a blessing. The modern video camera can often pick up candid comments as well as pictures which, as we all know, isn't always a good thing.

Singer sewing machines

Oh, there were other sewing machines, but nothing compared with the Singer. It sat there like a weird-looking occasional table until Mum flipped open the lid, which became the material table, then delved into the belly of the beast and pulled out the machine itself. It was dangerous — you had to keep your fingers clear of the flashing needle as it sewed furiously along the lowered hem on the legs of your winter pants. But the best bit was that you could turn the handle to operate it, as long as you stopped when Mum told you to.

That wasn't the only way to make the Singer go. You could operate it with your feet, leaving both hands free, by moving a treadmill plate up and down. This in turn moved a wheel, around which was a belt, which fitted into a smaller wheel on the end of the machine. I tell you, this was one great piece of engineering.

I liked to unhook the belt and would happily sit for hours, bouncing my feet on the treadmill to make that big old wheel spin like crazy. I don't know why it was such fun … it just was. They just don't make toys — sorry, I mean machines — like that any more.

The mangle

You know, the more I write this the more fun I realise all these items of drudgery were if you were a kid and not a grown-up. I'm sure not many women who spent every washday pushing their sheets and clothes through the mangle miss it for a minute. But I can still remember the thrill of pushing too much thickness of sheet through and having to pull on the handle with all my might to squeeze it … and the water squished out like a waterfall!

The downside was what mangles did to buttons, crushing them into little pieces — and always on your favourite shirt.

The copper

My mother loved her copper. She was a firm believer that to clean bed linen it required superheating almost to vapour. The copper would bubble away, sending the smell of hot soapy water for a radius of several streets. And of course, she boiled her Christmas puddings in it, wrapped in muslin. (The puddings were wrapped in muslin, not my mother — she's not that kind of mummy.) The smell ... ahh, as soon as I finish this, I'm off to make some custard.

The radiogram

These were just great. In all their mono, low-fidelity glory they could still make so much noise the neighbours thought there was an earthquake. The best were at least two metres long and waist-high. The radio dial glowed green and welcoming as you moved the tuner along with

Pterodactyl

Brontosaurus

T-Rex

a knob not much smaller than the big old wheel on the Singer. That the Beatles managed to sound new and exciting coming out of a piece of furniture like this is to their everlasting credit. Of course, the record-player played vinyl and bakelite records at 45, 33 or 78 r.p.m. What's an r.p.m.? This is where I came in, isn't it?

Don't fence me in

You can't overlook this Aussie icon, but you can look over it

The fence. Where would the great Aussie backyard be without the fence? It would have no beginning and no end, it would just be a bit of open space. There'd be nothing to look over to see what those strange noises coming from the neighbour's house are all about.

Admit it, we love a good fence. The richer (or more paranoid) we are, the bigger and stronger our fence. We've all heard the story of the three little pigs. Well, the true story is that around each of their houses they actually had fences. We all know what happened to the poor pig that built his fence of straw (brushwood), and the one that built his fence out of wood (palings). But the one that built his fence out of brick — well, he's still around and he's just put a couple of stone pigs either side of the gate.

It's strange that we insist on calling it a brick fence. The rest of the English-speaking world regards such a construction as a wall. If an Aussie had named the Great Wall of China, it'd now be the Great Brick Fence of China. Doesn't sound quite as impressive, does it?

Fences are made to keep people apart from their neighbours — or their neighbour's Rottweiler. Yet often they bring us together. There's that moment when you realise that your neighbour is in his backyard at the same time you are. You can avoid eye contact, which is totally acceptable, either respecting his privacy or wanting some yourself. Or you can give a hearty 'G'day', lean over the fence and see if he still has your rake that he borrowed last autumn.

There are many low-maintenance options, yet it seems that most of us still favour the traditional paling fence. Because it's made of timber, which various little chewy insects regard as lunch, we get another chance to bond over the fence — when we have to share the cost of replacing it. This is never done before it's too late, only after the fence crumbles into dust one morning as you put a cup of tea on the rail before pulling out a couple of weeds.

Ambitious handy types may even get together and repair the paling fence themselves. This will guarantee it will be a talking point with visitors for years to come, because fence building is a special trade and no amateur can do a comparable job. A handyman fence will always sag or bend or have palings which aren't plumb. You'll be able to see every dollar you saved on a fencing contractor for the next twenty years until the next set of borers finishes lunch.

I can remember an electric fence bringing my father and me together. We had dairy cows that we kept in the paddocks with two strands of electric fence wire. This was years ago, and the way the fence worked was with a couple of big car batteries and a transformer which sent an electric pulse down the wire every second. If a cow put its warm wet nose on the wire, it received a small electric charge. It wasn't high-voltage, but it was enough to keep the cow from trying to break out. My father was never keen to test it after he'd repaired it. Being young and fearless, I'd be the one who rested a piece of grass I was holding onto the wire to check that the fence was working again. The electric current would travel up the moisture in the grass and give me a little shock. My father reckoned that if it zapped me it would shock the cows, and if it didn't stun me it wouldn't stun the cows. Don't try this at home, particularly with a small piece of wet grass. Boy, did I learn that lesson the hard way.

Sadly, fences can also drive us apart. There are those amongst us who see the fence as the boundary between them and us, between good and evil, between green grass and greener grass. Bits of your beautiful trees which have dared to grow over their side of the fence are cut off and then dumped back over your side. Plants suddenly die and you discover their roots have been severed from the other side of the fence. Maybe the ultimate boundary dispute after the Great Brick Fence Of China was the Berlin Wall — sorry, Berlin Brick Fence. It kept the Berliners apart for about forty years until the people on the East side finally had the sense to say that enough was enough. Either that or somebody really wanted to get back the rake they'd lent to someone in West Berlin.

So don't let your fence keep you apart from the rest of humankind. Love it, admire it, grow climbers on it, paint it if you will, but remember that the people on the other side are just like you ... only with greener grass.

Never a dull moment

The long-lost joys of the summer holiday

The summer holiday has to be the greatest invention of all time, closely followed by the long weekend and sport. When we were very, very young, we didn't need a summer holiday because our whole lives were a holiday. But from the first day of school until now, the promise of those carefree summer weeks is the only thing that keeps us going.

Regular readers will know that I'm a mere forty-something years old and that it's not preying on my mind. I'm not like other writers. I'm not going to bore you with much reminiscing about how much better things were when I was younger — except to say that I cannot remember saying 'I'm bored' during my summer holidays. I can't believe I didn't, when I compare what we had to entertain us with our children's distractions.

Let's start at that favourite of all summer holiday spots, the beach. We had the bucket and spade, which were meant to indoctrinate us into a life of hard physical labour. It was our parents' clever way of keeping our expectations low. We were supposed to realise that the grander the sandcastle you try to build, the more likely it is to collapse or be kicked over by bigger kids. Which is why we learned quickly to include a few stones in the mix. There was no better sight on a hot summer's day than a mean old sandcastle-kicker hopping around clutching a throbbing big toe.

You still see the bucket and spade in use, but only by parents trying to entertain toddlers. As soon as kids are old enough to hold a Nintendo, they forget the delights of sand, sea and short-lived architecture. Blasting two-dimensional figures to smithereens is more fun and actually it's no less futile. But you did get a sense of achievement when you and twenty other kids built a sand-castle as big as a multi-storey car park. Apparently, the best feeling nowadays is beating Level 50 of a computer game.

Of course we had the traditional cricket bat and tennis ball, still seen today. And the beach ball, which I could see no point in at all until I was an adolescent and saw how good they looked in photographs when held by bikini-clad models — usually in ads that seemed to have nothing to do with bikinis, women or beach balls. We didn't have jet skis, so life was quieter, fish were calmer and sharks weren't as angry (though until *Jaws* they seemed much more scary). We didn't have sunblock and nobody seemed to be able to figure out why zinc cream on the nose and suntan lotion everywhere else didn't stop sunburn. But, of course, back then sunburn was as harmless as asbestos, cigarettes and nuclear testing in the Pacific.

The only mobile phones on view in those days were tin cans joined with a piece of string pulled taut between two boys dressed in swimming togs and plastic helmets, and carrying plastic machine-guns. Even if you tripped over the wire, they were much less annoying than today's cells phones and a lot less pretentious. When I was a kid, I never heard anyone on the beach saying, 'I'm bored, I think I'll give Rob a call.'

Away from the beach, we didn't have anywhere near the amount of wheeled goodies to keep us amused. Roller-skates just about rolled but, on anything other than the smoothest bitumen, progress was bumpy to say the least. Pogo-sticks were even bumpier.

Now there are in-line skates and skateboards, and half-pipes to use them in, not to mention all the groovy protective stuff to prevent the sort of constant abrasion which we just accepted. If a kid today had the scabs and bruises we routinely walked around with, Social Services would be knocking on the door quick-smart. I don't ride a bike these days because I'd feel ridiculous wearing a crash-hat on a pushbike. I don't think going over the handlebars did me any harm. You can hear those voices too, can't you?

As for theme parks, it was the zoo and Luna Park. I think the fact that Luna Park has flopped in this electronic age is proof that sliding down a piece of tin on a mat is not very exciting. It was once as terrifying as any roller-coaster at Australia's Wonderland.

Of course, our parents had even less to keep them amused than we did. My father, growing up in England, didn't go to the beach in case the Germans decided to storm the sea defences. He was never bored either, what with the sound of the bombs, air-raid warnings and anti-aircraft guns. If there was a lull, he could always play with his gas mask.

I'll tell you how lucky our kids are. My grandfather said that not only weren't there summer holidays when he was young, there weren't even summers.

The grander the sandcastle, the more likely it is to be kicked over by bigger kids

Epilogue

*I*f you're reading this, it means you've either read the book all the way through, or, like me, you start at the back of any publication you read, just in case there's a late-breaking sports story. If you have read it all the way through, I wish I could offer you some sort of prize, but there's no way of knowing if you were the first to get here, and as you know, there are no prizes for coming second. Except silver medals — sorry, none of those either.

My work continues, tucked away in the back of Better Homes and Gardens magazine. There's plenty more to write about. I can't see any major reconciliation between the sexes in the near future. It's not that we don't say 'Sorry' often enough, it's more that we don't know why we keep doing the things we have to say sorry for — sorry.

Meanwhile, the fuse on the powder-keg of discontent that is suburban man grows ever shorter. They tell us we don't need such big backyards. They tell us that medium density housing is the only sustainable future. They tell us that we have to embrace the idea of sub-division. Well, we've got a message for Them. We like great big cars and we vote. Phone now for your bumper sticker — 'Suburbanites do it in their own backyards'.